Speaking in Tongues

Speaking in Tongues

A Multidisciplinary Defense

TIMOTHY LAURITO

Foreword by Rick Dubose

WIPF & STOCK · Eugene, Oregon

SPEAKING IN TONGUES
A Multidisciplinary Defense

Wipf & Stock
An Imprint of Wipf and Stock Publishers
199 W. 8th Ave., Suite 3
Eugene, OR 97401

www.wipfandstock.com

PAPERBACK ISBN: 978-1-6667-1387-9
HARDCOVER ISBN: 978-1-6667-1388-6
EBOOK ISBN: 978-1-6667-1389-3

OCTOBER 19, 2021

For my sons Judah, Asher, and Adon.
I am incredibly proud of you.
I pray that no matter what else you may do,
you will grow up to be Spirit-filled men of God.

Contents

Foreword

THE HOLY SPIRIT'S WORK is first revealed to us as a covering womb over the earth during creation. He provided the controlling atmosphere as the Father's word was sent to build creation design upon design and layer upon layer. Once completed, God declared his creation work very good and finished. The work of the Spirit, however, was not finished. He continues working all through the Old Testament. He anoints prophets, priests, and kings. He shows up as fire before Moses, in a cloud of fire before Israel, and as fire to Gideon, to David, and at Solomon's temple dedication. His fire transformed the natural work of sacrificial offerings into spiritually acceptable atonement and the normal work of men into Spirit-empowered action. The last time we see the Holy Spirit as fire is in the book of Acts chapter 2. There, the Spirit manifested as fire resting on the disciples as a single tongue of fire on each of them. The result of these fire tongues was that they spoke in tongues (Acts 2:4). While we never see the Spirit as fire again, we continue to see the Spirit manifested through Spirit-baptized people who speak in tongues.

I will never forget one Sunday at the church Rita and I pastored in Sachse, Texas, when the Spirit interrupted our morning service. The sanctuary was packed, and as the worship filled the house, the atmosphere the Spirit provided was electric. I was standing up front, worshiping along with everyone else, waiting my turn to take the microphone after the last song on the list. As the worship leader led the mood from exuberant celebration to a a more personal, quieter, more introspective moment, there was a mournful and severe, almost heavy, interruption—someone speaking in tongues!

You see, we believe in the gifts of the Spirit and had taught on them and made room for the Holy Spirit to led us by his gifts as he saw fit in every gathering, Sunday morning included. So, this was not out of the ordinary for us, and our people knew how to respond. We all sensed this was a genuine act of God that needed no correction. All we needed now was an interpretation. As I stood there, I began to feel, sense, and hear the Holy Spirit speak a word directly into my heart, but I knew giving it would be risky because it was so personal. Yet, I knew that voice and knew it was the Holy Spirit, so I stepped to the microphone and began to speak in English what I believed God wanted to say to his people.

The interpretation was directed to someone planning to commit suicide that day and even described their preparation and plans. The Spirit told them that he had a better plan for them and that it was God who had led them into this Pentecostal church service. After the interpretation, I led the church into a time of prayer for the person. We bound the purposes of Satan and prayed for the person to be free from fear and death. Then I had everyone bow their heads to give privacy to the individual to whom the Holy Spirit spoke. I then asked the person to identify themselves. A well-dressed, professional-looking woman looked straight at me and raised her hand all the way from the second row in the back. I said, "God just interrupted this service because he loves you and because right now you are the most important person in this building. He has a plan for your life and he can fix whatever problems have brought you to this bad decision." She came forward and met me at the altar area, and I lead her in a prayer of surrender and faith as we prayed over her and laid hands on her. She wept her way through to joy and freedom.

Later, after the service was over, I sat down with her and listened to her story. At the end of her story, she said, "I told God I would give him one more chance and that I would go back to church one more time. I thought this was a normal evangelical church; I didn't know it was Pentecostal when I came in. But after a few moments, I knew it was different; I could feel it. Then that powerful speaking in tongues started, and your explanation and interpretation of it came. I knew it was real." Her next statement hit me like a ton of bricks. She said, "You know, if I had not come to a Pentecostal church, I would be dead by now!"

I will never forget that service or her statement. For it was because of the Holy Spirit working through his gifts that this woman's life and soul were both saved that day. What took place did not occur through the sermon I preached that morning but through the Spirit-directed manifestation of his gifts. While certainly sermons and their preachers matter, they do not replace the gifts of the Spirit being in operation within the church today.

Dr. Laurito's book helps us understand the Holy Spirit's connection to speaking in tongues as the initial evidence of Spirit baptism, communicative language to God, and the manifestation of the Holy Spirit's work in the church. Read this work carefully and learn how speaking in tongues works and why God chose tongues as the evidence of Spirit baptism.

Rev. Rick DuBose
Assistant General Superintendent
Assemblies of God USA

Preface

You picked up a book about speaking in tongues! Since you are reading this, I assume that you are interested in the phenomenon of tongue speech at some level. Whether you are someone who practices the phenomenon, someone who would like to experience it, or someone who simply has questions about the validity of the practice, this book has something for you. While this book is primarily designed to equip self-identified Pentecostals in their ability to defend their practice of speaking in tongues, this resource could also prove helpful in helping non-Pentecostals to recognize the value and validity of speaking in other tongues.

Admittedly, speaking in tongues is a strange phenomenon! Given its inherently odd nature, what would cause people to practice the phenomenon enthusiastically? How is it that such a peculiar act could provide any spiritual value? Can the act of speaking in other tongues stand up to scientific scrutiny? Is speaking in tongues just the psychobabble of religious fanaticism, or is there more to the experience? Should the phenomenon still be practiced within the modern church, and if so, how should it function? These are all legitimate questions that contemporary Pentecostalism must address.

As someone who has actively practiced the phenomenon for over two decades, my personal experience with speaking in tongues has been something that I have deeply cherished. However, as a young practitioner of speaking in tongues, I distinctly remember feeling wholly inadequate in my ability to explain what was taking place through tongue speech. While I never doubted the fact that something spiritual was happening through the act of speaking in tongues, what exactly was taking place through glossolalic speech was something I could not explain. As I continued my glossolalic practice, it became painfully evident to me that I was not alone in this struggle to make sense of the practice of speaking in tongues. The giant elephant in the Pentecostal Church is the fact that a significant percentage of Pentecostal adherents identify with my experience (more on this in chapter 6). The truth of the matter is that while Pentecostals believe in the practice of speaking in tongues and deeply cherish the culture of Pentecostalism, if honest, many Pentecostals feel a deep sense of inadequacy in being able to defend their practice of speaking in tongues.

If you can identify with my experience, let me encourage you that you are not alone. To the person looking to be better equipped to defend the purpose and practice of speaking in tongues, this book is for you. For the person struggling with questions regarding the validity of speaking in tongues, this is a no-fluff book designed to answer your questions. Whether you are new to the phenomenon of speaking in tongues or have been a practitioner for a long time, this book will challenge and deepen your thinking about the subject of speaking in tongues.

Introduction

WHILE THE SUBJECT OF speaking in tongues has garnered much attention throughout the last century, little work has been done to examine the
phenomenon from a multidisciplinary approach. Further, those who have
done so have written to an academic audience, not the average Pentecostal
adherent. This book is designed to bridge that gap and provide everyday
Pentecostals with a resource that will give them a more profound framework to understand their unique practice of speaking in tongues.

The advantage of a multidisciplinary approach to speaking in tongues
is that it offers the practitioner multiple lenses to view the phenomenon.
The result of this method is that Pentecostals are equipped with a broad
foundation from which they can build their practice of speaking in other
tongues. From a biblical/theological perspective of speaking in tongues,
the Pentecostal can recognize the scriptural foundation for the practice of
tongue speech. From the standpoint of practical theology, the Pentecostal
can see the everyday implications of speaking in tongues upon the practitioner. From a social science perspective, the Pentecostal is afforded the
opportunity to understand how speaking in tongues "speaks" to the fields
of linguistics, psychology, and sociology. Finally, from a historical analysis
perspective, the Pentecostal can trace the historicity of the phenomenon
and is granted a greater context for understanding its current usage. These
various disciplines have something unique to offer the Pentecostal adherent in understanding the value of speaking in tongues. In addition, a multidisciplinarian examination of speaking in tongues provides Pentecostals
with a wide range of tools in defending their distinctive practice from those
who would reject it as a valid practice.

The book's structure is designed to prioritize the biblical/theological
defense of speaking in tongues. Therefore, it is encouraged that the book be

read in the order presented. However, the advantage of a multidisciplinary approach is that each chapter is distinct and can be read independently of the other chapters. Whether you start at chapter 1 and work your way systematically through the book or start at a particular chapter of interest and then circle back, the purpose of this resource is to equip Pentecostal adherents in their ability to defend their practice of speaking in tongues. In addition to arming the Pentecostal with an apologetic of speaking in tongues, this book is designed to empower the practitioner of speaking in tongues to more deeply enjoy the glorious wonders afforded them through Spirit-inspired tongue speech.

As the differentiating doctrine that distinguishes Pentecostalism, speaking in tongues must be understood by Pentecostal adherents if the movement is expected to continue. While Pentecostalism has grown leaps and bounds over the past century, could it be that while achieving larger crowds and more adherents, Pentecostalism has failed to train those who self-identify as Pentecostals on the purpose and function of speaking in tongues? In chapter 6, empirical research conducted by the author examines Pentecostal adherents' knowledge of and attitudes toward the subject of speaking in tongues. The results of this research should give the Pentecostal Church pause to reevaluate our methods of training adherents in the doctrine and practice of speaking in other tongues.

In an effort to be proactive in this growing problem, this book is designed to equip self-identified Pentecostals in their ability to defend their unique practice of speaking in tongues. Additionally, for those Pentecostal adherents who have never experienced speaking in tongues, this resource is intended to aid them in understanding the purpose of Spirit-inspired speech. The truth is that what one generation holds as a belief but fails to practice, the next generation will neither believe nor practice. Therefore, for Pentecostalism to continue to grow, its adherents must be equipped to defend their distinctive belief and empowered to practice the phenomenon of speaking in tongues.

1

A Lukan Theology
of Speaking in Tongues

INTRODUCTION

As a personal witness to both the ministry of Jesus and the exploits of the early church, Luke writes to Theophilus to provide an accurate account of the Spirit of God's activity in this world. The working of the Spirit within the Luke-Acts narrative reveals that the author possesses a dynamic theology of the Spirit. The Lukan description of the Spirit's character communicates the fact that he possesses personhood and initiates divine purposes. At every critical point in Luke's two-volume account, the Spirit can be found to play a central role. At the incarnation (Luke 1:35), Jesus' baptism (Luke 3:22), the beginning of his ministry (Luke 4:1), the Upper Room (Acts 2:4), and the acceptance of the Gentiles (Acts 10:44–48), the Spirit is central to Luke's narrative. This action of the Spirit in Luke-Acts is not passive but is dynamic in its power. For example, the Lukan record depicts the Spirit working to reveal (Luke 2:26), guide (Luke 4:1), give power (Luke 4:14; Acts 1:8), anoint (Luke 4:18), teach (Luke 12:12), speak (Acts 4:25; 8:29; 10:19; 11:12; 13:2; 21:11), prohibit (Acts 16:7), and testify (Acts 20:23).

Although separated within the biblical canon, Luke-Acts was designed to be a single two-volume work by the author. New Testament scholar W. C. van Unnik writes:

> We speak of it (Luke-Acts) as a unit. . . . It is generally accepted that
> both books have a common author; the possibility that the Gospel
> and the Acts do not belong together is not seriously discussed. By

almost unanimous consent they are considered to be two volumes of a single work.[1]

The Holy Spirit—within all the New Testament writings—is fundamentally the work of the empowering activity of God (2 Tim 3:16–17). Yet, Luke's exceptional attention to the work of the Spirit in his writings is powerfully evident; for the Luke-Acts connection reveals an emphasis by the author to link the work of the Spirit in both books. From Luke's first reference to the Spirit in the angelic prophecy of John's birth (Luke 1:15) to the promise of Christ to send power from on high to his disciples (Luke 24:49), the Gospel of Luke is filled with references to the importance of the Spirit in the life of Christ followers. Throughout his earthly ministry, Jesus prophesied that the Holy Spirit would be given to those who asked (Luke 11:13), empower those who were filled (Luke 24:49), and assist those who were put on trial (Luke 12:11, 12). As such, it is evident that Jesus saw the necessity of the Holy Spirit directly in terms of accomplishing kingdom purposes. Similarly, Luke views the primary role of the Spirit in relation to the kingdom of God as the power for proclaiming the kingdom.[2]

Given Luke's primary emphasis on the Spirit's work in the life of Christ, it should come as no surprise that Luke's second work also centers around the Spirit's activities. This theme permeates the book of Acts and begins with the outpouring of the Spirit upon the disciples on the day of Pentecost (Acts 2). So significant is the day of Pentecost in Luke's account that it can be seen as the central event in his narrative. Historically and theologically, as well as locationally in Luke's narration, this event comes in the middle—between his account of the Christ event on the one hand and his history of the spread of the gospel throughout the Roman Empire on the other hand.[3] It is precisely at this critical midpoint that Luke's narrative describes the fulfillment of Christ's promise of Spirit baptism (Acts 1:5) for the expressed purpose of empowered witness (Acts 1:8).

In approaching the Acts of the Apostles, a Lukan focus on the Spirit is of no surprise. However, what is surprising is that the phenomenon of glossolalia (speaking in tongues) is a foundational thread associated with the arrival of the Spirit's baptism (Acts 2, 8, 10, 19). Christ's prophecy concerning the Spirit's indwelling (Luke 24:49; Acts 1:4) offered no indications of glossolalic activity as part of the Spirit-baptism experience. Yet, the fact

1. Unnik, "Luke-Acts," 100.

2. Cho, "Primary Role of the Spirit," 197.

3. Wyckoff, "Baptism," 153.

that Christ does not disclose the role of speaking in tongues within Spirit baptism does nothing to negate its unmistakable presence within the fulfillment of his promise. While Christ did not explain the sign (glossolalia) of Spirit baptism or the when (day of Pentecost), he clearly explains the why (missional empowerment). Therefore, while the disciples could not envision the events that would shortly come to pass, Christ's missional-empowerment focus in Spirit baptism points to the fact that whatever was about to come would be transformational in its power. To this point, Stronstad explains:

> The Pentecost narrative introduces both the future mission of the disciples and the complementary empowering of the Spirit. The Pentecost narrative is the story of the transfer of the charismatic Spirit from Jesus to the disciples. In other words, having become the exclusive bearer of the Holy Spirit at his baptism, Jesus becomes the giver of the Spirit at Pentecost.[4]

Therefore, the Lukan theology of Spirit baptism can be defined simply as the Spirit's empowering witness of Christ. Luke records this central point through the message of Peter to the Gentile Cornelius: "How God anointed Jesus of Nazareth with the Holy Spirit and with power. He went about doing good and healing all who were oppressed by the devil, for God was with him" (Acts 10:38). Therefore, a Lukan theology of the Holy Spirit begins within a framework of understanding that it is the same Spirit of empowering witness that resided within Christ that has now been imparted to the disciples on the day of Pentecost. What Pentecostals seek to note within the Spirit's impartment of empowering witness is that the presence of speaking in tongues appears to be the first external sign of this supernatural phenomenon.

This chapter will examine a Lukan theology of speaking in tongues with a particular focus on how speaking in tongues is connected to initial physical evidence and what role the phenomenon should have within the church today. To accomplish this task, a critical integrative analysis of the events of the day of Pentecost (Acts 2), the miracle with the Samaritan believers (Acts 8), the Spirit baptism of Cornelius and his household (Acts 10), and the outpouring of the Spirit on the Ephesian disciples (Acts 19) will be examined in order to discover a wholistic interpretation of a Lukan theology of speaking in tongues.

---

4. Stronstad, *Charismatic Theology*, 55.

THE DAY OF PENTECOST

Acts 2:1–12

> When the day of Pentecost had come, they were all together in one place. And suddenly there came from heaven a noise like a violent rushing wind, and it filled the whole house where they were sitting. And there appeared to them tongues as of fire distributing themselves, and they rested on each one of them. And they were all filled with the Holy Spirit and began to speak with other tongues, as the Spirit was giving them utterance. Now there were Jews living in Jerusalem, devout men from every nation under heaven. And when this sound occurred, the crowd came together, and were bewildered because each one of them was hearing them speak in his own language. They were amazed and astonished, saying, "Why, are not all these who are speaking Galileans? And how is it that we each hear them in our own language to which we were born? Parthians and Medes and Elamites, and residents of Mesopotamia, Judea and Cappadocia, Pontus and Asia, Phrygia and Pamphylia, Egypt and the districts of Libya around Cyrene, and visitors from Rome, both Jews and proselytes, Cretans and Arabs—we hear them in our own tongues speaking of the mighty deeds of God." And they all continued in amazement and great perplexity, saying to one another, "What does this mean?"

The day of Pentecost serves as a critical instance of research for a Lukan theology of speaking in tongues. Not only because it is the first occurrence but because it emphasizes speaking in tongues to be the initial physical evidence of Holy Spirit baptism and relevant for the church today. Upon the arrival of the day of Pentecost, the disciples were waiting at Jerusalem to receive the outpouring of the Holy Spirit in obedience to the commands of Christ (Acts 1:4). The pilgrimage festival of Pentecost (Weeks) was the second of the three great harvest festivals of Judaism, taking place between Passover and Tabernacles. In the Old Testament, Pentecost is referred to as the Festival of Weeks and was a celebration of the wheat harvest.[5] This feast would occur seven weeks after Passover on the sixth day of Sivan (Exod 23:14–17). F. F. Bruce summarizes the importance of this feast by stating:

> The day of Pentecost was so called because it fell on the fiftieth day after the presentation of the first sheaf to be reaped of the barley

5. Polhill, *Acts*, 97.

harvest, that is, the fiftieth day from the first Sunday after Passover (πεντηκοστῆς being the Greek word for "fiftieth").[6]

In describing the supernatural phenomenon that took place on this occasion, Luke divides the celestial visitation of the Spirit into three distinct but simultaneous events. These events include a sudden hurricane-like sound originating from heaven (Acts 2:2), the individual appearance of fire-like tongues on all the believers (Acts 2:3), and the infilling of the Holy Spirit, which resulted in Spirit-directed speech in other tongues (Acts 2:4). The first two signs of the Spirit's arrival were visible, external forces. However, the last sign of speaking in tongues was an internal force making itself visible and signified the Spirit's indwelling within the disciples. This distinction is important because, while the hurricane-like sound and the fire-like tongues are never repeated in association with Spirit baptism, the internal sign of Spirit indwelling (as evidenced by speaking in tongues) is repeated throughout the Acts of the Apostles.

Luke is quite clear that upon receiving the Holy Spirit, *all* the disciples gathered in the Upper Room, were filled with the Holy Spirit and spoke with other tongues (Acts 2:4). It was the external sign of glossolalia that signified the Spirit's internal infilling. Stanley Horton says, "Only one sign was a part of the Pentecostal baptism. All who were filled with the Holy Spirit began to speak with other tongues as the Spirit enabled them. That is, they used their tongues, their muscles, they spoke."[7] Thus, Luke plainly describes that the visible sign of the Holy Spirit's arrival on the day of Pentecost was the disciples' ability to speak boldly in an unknown tongue through the direction of the Spirit.

Speaking in Tongues as Initial Physical Evidence

While not universally accepted by all within the Pentecostal movement, the classical Pentecostal position of initial physical evidence means that Pentecostals expect speaking in tongues as the external marker of the reception of Spirit baptism. From a classical Pentecostal perspective, this outward sign is speaking in tongues. The earliest reference to speaking in tongues being

6. Bruce, *Book of Acts*, 49.

7. Horton, *What the Bible Says*, 143.

called the "initial evidence" is in the Statement of Fundamental Truths of the Assembly of God, composed and adopted in 1916.[8]

We should not overlook the fact that the phenomenon of speaking in tongues was the first external sign to the diaspora Jews at Pentecost that something supernatural of the Spirit had occurred. Because Luke places the disciples' speech as being before the gathering crowds, this suggests that it was speaking in tongues that served as the "sign" to others that a Spirit-indwelling moment had occurred.[9] The glossolalic utterances of the disciples on the day of Pentecost not only served as the catalyst which brought about awareness of the Spirit's arrival, but it also served as a visible testimony to his work of Spirit baptism. Since this is the case, it is logical to conclude that Luke intended that the initial sign of the Spirit's indwelling of those at Pentecost was that they spoke in other tongues. Carl Brumback agrees with the clarity of the Acts 2 text:

> There can be no question in any unprejudiced mind that the fact which this narrative sets before us is, that the disciples began to speak in various languages. All attempts to evade this are connected with some forcing of the text, or some far-fetched and indefensible explanation.[10]

Without question, speaking in tongues was not simply one of many signs of Spirit baptism but was *the* sign to the gathered crowd that something supernatural had occurred. Just as with other divine acts, there is a physical, evidential component to the event of Pentecost—namely, speaking in tongues.

The revelatory work of the Spirit within humanity does not happen independently of human awareness of that work. That is to say, God has designed that the experiential workings of divine presence through the Spirit be done in such a way that humanity is cognitive of this action. Therefore, any attempt to strip the externally visible sign of speaking in other tongues is to miss a significant factor in Luke's description of the day of Pentecost. The manifestation of speaking in tongues as an external sign of the Holy Spirit's arrival is but the first instance of the biblical precedent for speaking in tongues as the initial physical evidence of baptism in the Holy Spirit. It is abundantly clear that Luke intended his readers to understand that Spirit

8. "Brief History," para. 5. The 1916 Statement of Fundamental Truths can be found through the Flower Pentecostal Heritage Center: https://ifphc.org/.

9. Mills, *Theological/Exegetical Approach*, 62.

10. Brumback, *Tongues*, 43.

baptism was available to—and indeed, should be experienced by—every believer.

From a Pentecostal perspective, the Spirit came upon the disciples at Pentecost not as the source of salvific work but rather as the source of power for effective witness. For this reason, Pentecostals describe Spirit baptism as an experience distinct from conversion which unleashes a new dimension of the Spirit's power—one which is repeatedly marked in Luke's account by the presence of speaking in other tongues.

Speaking in Tongues for the Church Today

In contrast to the Pentecostal view that all spiritual manifestations of the Spirit are still in operation today, some Christians hold to a cessationist belief concerning the gifts of the Spirit. Cessationism teaches that the spiritual gifts outlined in Scripture have now ceased their operation within the church and are no longer needed. Jimmy Jividen outlines the position of the cessationist by stating, "The *glossa* gift in the New Testament—along with other miraculous signs—served their purpose and passed away. What is passing for the *glossa* gift today is no more than a psychological phenomenon which finds expression in ecstatic utterances."[11]

The cessationists argue that the baptism of the Holy Spirit at Pentecost was not a subsequent work to salvation for the disciples but an inextricable part of salvation for the disciples. Merrill Unger argues for this position:

> The baptism of the Spirit at Pentecost was not a second experience of power, but a vital and inseparable part of the so great salvation Jesus purchased by His redemption on the cross. Hence the only relation of Pentecost's tongues to the baptism of the Spirit is that those saved so spoke, the baptism being a part of their salvation not an experience subsequent to it.[12]

However, this position originates from a false assumption that the church was "born" on the day of Pentecost. A closer examination of Scripture reveals that the church began much earlier than the events that took place in Acts 2.

After the resurrection of Christ, Jesus appeared to the disciples who were hiding behind closed doors out of fear. He said, "Peace be with you;

11. Jividen, *Glossolalia*, 144.
12. Unger, *Teachings on Tongues*, 29.

as the Father has sent Me, I also send you" (John 20:21). These words of evangelistic commission to the disciples were immediately followed by Christ breathing on them and commanding, "Receive the Holy Spirit. If you forgive the sins of any, their sins have been forgiven them; if you retain the sins of any, they have been retained" (John 20:23). This passage presents an ecclesiological paradigm for the origins of the church before the Day of Pentecost, distinguished by two aspects.

First, it is evident that the purpose of Christ's breathing (ἐνεφύσησεν) upon the disciples was to accomplish a supernatural work of the Spirit. Consequently, this very same Greek word is used in the Septuagint, as God breathed the breath of life into Adam (Gen 2:7). Moreover, just as in the case of Adam, this supernatural breathing was not merely a symbolic act. Rather, it was an actual impartation of the divine Spirit of God. Since Christ had been crucified, risen, and glorified, the regenerative life of the Spirit—made possible through faith in Christ—was now able to be administered to Christ's disciples.

To further substantiate the salvific nature of Christ's breathing on the disciples, we see that Christ prophesied that when the Spirit did come, he would dwell within them: "That is the Spirit of truth, whom the world cannot receive, because it does not see Him or know Him, but you know Him because He abides with you and will be in you" (John 14:17). The glorious transition of the Spirit from being *with* the disciples to being *within* the disciples predates the work of the Spirit on the day of Pentecost. This well-defined depiction of Spirit indwelling, post-resurrection and pre-Pentecost, reveals an undeniable regenerative work of the Spirit within the disciples which precedes their Spirit baptism on the day of Pentecost.

Secondly, it is quite clear from the words of Christ that the reason for breathing (ἐνεφύσησεν) Spirit life into the disciples was for salvific purposes. The life of the Spirit being breathed into the disciples enabled them to now be facilitators of Christ's atoning work of salvation. Yet, how can this be possible if they were not first recipients of that atoning work themselves? The obvious answer is that since this event immediately follows the resurrection of Christ, it is logical to assert that this moment of Jesus breathing upon them was in fact a regenerative moment for the disciples, as previously ascertained. From these two indicators, an ecclesiological case can be made that the church was already in existence prior to the Spirit baptism which took place on the day of Pentecost.

At this point, it should be noted that simply because the disciples experienced a subsequent work of the Spirit prior to Acts 2, this does nothing to diminish the work of the Spirit upon regeneration. Instead, Spirit baptism should be seen to facilitate the continual deepening of the Spirit's work in the believer's life. The Pentecostal's insistence that Luke teaches a subsequent work of the Spirit after salvation in no way suggests a minimizing of the salvific work of the Spirit.

In attempting to minimize the significance of the disciples' salvific experience in John 20:22, James Dunn writes, "We cannot simply assume that the Gospels and Acts are all bare historical narratives which complement each other in a direct 1:1 ratio; nor can we assume that Luke and John have the same emphases and aims."[13] While this argument is valid in some cases, it is invalid when comparing John (John 20:22) and Luke (Acts 2) because the emphases and aims of both writers are to explain the impetus of the Spirit's arrival. In both cases, the biblical author is seeking to explain the operation of the Spirit in the life of the followers of Christ. Additionally, some critics argue that biblical narratives teach us only about God's actions in the past, and they are not meant to provide us with models for our responses to God. However, this is clearly not the way that Jesus or the Apostles viewed the function of biblical narratives. Both Jesus and the apostles used Old Testament narratives to teach essential truths regarding faith and obedience to God.[14]

The fact remains that the cessationist position concerning the ceasing of spiritual manifestations is not consistent with what the early church believed. Peter, preaching to the questioning crowd that had gathered in response to the Spirit's work on the day of Pentecost, states:

> For these men are not drunk, as you suppose, for it is *only* the third hour of the day; but this is what was spoken of through the prophet Joel: "And it shall be in the last days," God says, "That I will pour forth of My Spirit on all mankind; And your sons and your daughters shall prophesy, and your young men shall see visions, and your old men shall dream dreams; Even on My bondslaves, both men and women, I will in those days pour forth of My Spirit, and they shall prophesy." (Acts 2:15–18)

These words of explanation regarding the outpouring of the Spirit reveal that Peter believed that Spirit baptism was intended to be for all the church,

13. Dunn, *Baptism*, 39.

14. Keener, *Spirit Hermeneutics*, 23.

both past and present. There is no hint that Peter views the events of Pentecost as being intended to be available for a limited few, for a limited time, at the beginning of church history.

While the Spirit's initial arrival was obviously a one-time event, his impact and influence were never intended to be limited to the early church. To confirm that the working of the Spirit must continue past this time to the return of the Lord, Peter prophetically recites the words of the prophet Joel:

> It will come about after this that I will pour out My Spirit on all mankind; and your sons and daughters will prophesy, your old men will dream dreams, your young men will see visions. Even on the male and female servants I will pour out My Spirit in those days. I will display wonders in the sky and on the earth, blood, fire and columns of smoke. The sun will be turned into darkness and the moon into blood before the great and awesome day of the Lord comes. (Joel 2:28–31)

It is evident that both the prophet Joel and Peter view these signs as being in reference to eschatological (end-time) events. This connection signifies that the work and gifts of the Holy Spirit (as manifested on the day of Pentecost) have a purpose for the entirety of the church age and not just the early days of the apostles.

Roger Stronstad addresses Peter's understanding of the continual function of the baptism of the Holy Spirit:

> As Luke's history of the spread of Christianity shows, as a being baptized in the Holy Spirit kind of experience, new disciples will continue to be baptized in the Holy Spirit. Clearly, Peter understood it correctly. The Father's promise given through John the Baptist about being baptized in the Holy Spirit is for the first generation of disciples, their children, namely, the second generation, and, indeed, for all who are afar off.[15]

As such, Luke's account of the early church reveals that being baptized in the Holy Spirit, as evidenced by speaking in tongues, was intended to continue throughout the generations of the church. Starting with the events on the day of Pentecost, each Lukan account of Spirit baptism builds an unmistakable pattern that reveals a divine purpose for the use of speaking in tongues. To this point Amos Yong writes:

---

15. Stronstad, "On Being Baptized," 173.

This gift of the spirit was promised by the Father (Luke 24:49; Acts 1:4) to empower witness to the world about God's deeds of power (Acts 2:11). Even as Acts 1:8 structures the arc of the narrative so that the spirit-empowered witness travels from Jerusalem (Acts 2:1–5:11) through Judea (Acts 5:12–8:3) and Samaria (Acts 8:4–25) and on to the ends of the earth (Acts 8:26–28:31), effectively arriving in Rome (Acts 28:11–31), literally the edge of the known world from an Israel-centered point of view, the initial pentecostal outpouring was given. . . . What we have here is a primordial form of reverse mission, the unexpected phenomenon whereby the local Galilean messianists not only proclaim the good news to the world at their doors but are transformed by the witness that comes in and through these other languages.[16]

Luke's description of the manifestation of the Holy Spirit on the day of Pentecost introduces a Lukan theology on the purpose and function of speaking in tongues. Since the purpose of the Spirit's arrival at Pentecost was not soteriological, the events establish a clear biblical precedent for speaking in tongues as the initial physical evidence of Holy Spirit baptism. Additionally, Peter's explanation of this event reveals that speaking in tongues is meant to remain a sign of Spirit baptism for the church today. While the historical advent of the Holy Spirit's emergence at Pentecost was a one-time event, the results of this event were never intended to be limited to one generation of people or group. This is evident by the fact that from the first time the Spirit was poured out, speaking in tongues was present, and this pattern continues to be repeated throughout Luke's account.

WHAT DID SIMON SEE?

Acts 8:14–25

> Now when the apostles in Jerusalem heard that Samaria had received the word of God, they sent them Peter and John, who came down and prayed for them that they might receive the Holy Spirit. For He had not yet fallen upon any of them; they had simply been baptized in the name of the Lord Jesus. Then they began laying their hands on them, and they were receiving the Holy Spirit. Now when Simon saw that the Spirit was bestowed through the laying on of the apostles' hands, he offered them money, saying, "Give

16. Yong, *Mission after Pentecost*, 172.

this authority to me as well, so that everyone on whom I lay my hands may receive the Holy Spirit." But Peter said to him, "May your silver perish with you, because you thought you could obtain the gift of God with money! You have no part or portion in this matter, for your heart is not right before God. Therefore repent of this wickedness of yours, and pray the Lord that, if possible, the intention of your heart may be forgiven you. For I see that you are in the gall of bitterness and in the bondage of iniquity." But Simon answered and said, "Pray to the Lord for me yourselves, so that nothing of what you have said may come upon me." So, when they had solemnly testified and spoken the word of the Lord, they started back to Jerusalem, and were preaching the gospel to many villages of the Samaritans.

Of the accounts that Luke provides concerning the subject of speaking in tongues, the case of what took place with the Samaritan believers has been the subject of much discussion and debate. The narrative compels the reader to address the chronological separation between the salvific faith of the Samaritans and their reception of the Holy Spirit. Stronstad explains the importance of these issues:

> Not only did their faith fail to affect the reception of the Spirit, but their baptism likewise failed to be the locus of their reception of the Spirit. This is a vexing theological problem for many interpreters, for it contradicts their theological presupposition concerning the baptism of the Holy Spirit.[17]

In addition to the Samaritan case presenting the problem of Spirit reception after salvation, Luke also, unlike any of the other three accounts of Spirit baptism (Acts 2, 10, 19), chooses not to disclose the specific manifestation of the Spirit. This ambiguity has resulted in an ongoing attempt to understand what precisely Simon saw when Peter and John prayed for these converts to be baptized in the Holy Spirit. Thus, while Luke provides undeniable evidence that some outwardly observable manifestation occurred in association with the Samaritan disciples receiving the Holy Spirit, he remains silent on what was apparent to all those who observed. However, Luke's silence does not mean we cannot arrive at an accurate understanding of what took place in Samaria.

This section will examine Luke's development of the events at Samaria. The analysis reveals that these believers received the baptism of the Holy

17. Stronstad, *Charismatic Theology*, 72.

Spirit *after* their conversion and that the manifestation of the Spirit was speaking in tongues. Furthermore, this section on the events in Samaria will further establish the importance of speaking in tongues as the initial physical evidence of Spirit baptism and as a relevant spiritual manifestation for the church today.

Speaking in Tongues as Initial Physical Evidence

From Luke's account, there can be no doubt that a visible manifestation occurred among the Samaritan believers which indicated that they had received the Holy Spirit. However, Luke is silent on what that manifestation was. The issue then debated by scholars in this account is this: What was the visible manifestation that Simon saw the Samaritans receive?

It is first essential to understand the immediate context of what Simon had already witnessed when asking this question. As a recent convert to Christianity (possibly at the same time as the other Samaritans), Simon has already wondered at the signs and miracles that Philip performed during his preaching (Acts 8:13). Simon, who was previously a magician and well-versed in the enchantment of sorcerous wonders, knew that what Philip was doing had its origin in the supernatural. However, what happened to the Samaritans through the ministry of Peter and John was different. This new miracle created a lustful desire within Simon to possess its potential for himself.

Some have suggested that what Simon saw (and thus desired) was simply the Samaritans prophesying or exhibiting ecstatic utterances. However, these explanations seem wholly inadequate when one considers that Simon was willing to pay money for the power to give this manifestation that he saw to others. Prophecy would not have been a novelty to Simon, and ecstatic utterances would hardly have been worth Simon's money, since he already knew how to mesmerize a crowd (Acts 8:9–11). Furthermore, if we compare the amazement of the crowd on the day of Pentecost (Acts 2:12) to how Simon marveled at what he saw the Samaritans receive, it is logical to assert that the outward, visible manifestation exhibited by the Samaritans that Simon saw and desired was glossolalia. F. F. Bruce also arrives at this same conclusion, stating, "The context (of the Samaritan case of baptism in Holy Spirit) leaves us in no doubt that their reception of the

attended by an external manifestation such as had marked His
the earliest disciples at Pentecost."[18]

...tionally, some have argued that because Luke is silent concerning speaking in tongues in this text, this serves as proof that this spiritual manifestation should not be required as a sign of Spirit baptism. Those questioning speaking in tongues as the sign of Spirit baptism ask why, if Luke intended to teach evidential tongues as normative, he does not present tongues as the immediate result of Spirit baptism in the case of the Samaritans' Spirit baptism. Yet, an argument from silence in this particular case does nothing to weaken the overall pattern of speaking in tongues throughout Luke's accounts of Spirit baptisms in Acts. Addressing this objection, Stanley Horton writes:

> Luke often does not explain everything when it is clear elsewhere.
> For example, he does not mention water baptism every time he
> tells about people believing or being added to the Church, but it is
> clear that the failure to mention this is not significant.[19]

Luke's silence regarding speaking in tongues in the case of the Samaritan believers does nothing to negate its overall importance. Neither does it refute the biblical pattern of speaking in tongues being the initial physical evidence of Spirit baptism throughout Acts (Acts 2, 10, 19). Instead, the context justifies the presence of speaking in tongues, since the temporal separation between conversion and Spirit baptism—as is clearly evident in the Samaritan account—fits the other narratives of Spirit baptism. Therefore, when taken in the context of the entirety of Luke's narrative, it is not ambiguous what happened to the Samaritans when they received the Holy Spirit. They spoke in other tongues.

While Luke does not set out to produce a theology of Spirit baptism in his account that deliberately tries to demonstrate that "tongues" is the initial physical evidence of Spirit baptism, this does not make the doctrine invalid given the fact that within his narrative, Luke continually portrays speaking in tongues as accompanying Spirit baptism. In other words, Luke's purpose for his account is not primarily to set forth a systematic theology of any particular doctrine. However, this reality should not prevent Christians from drawing theological truths from Luke's narrative account in the Acts of the Apostles of how the Spirit worked.

18. Bruce, "Book of Acts," 181.
19. Horton, *Book of Acts*, 106.

Therefore, while speaking in tongues is not explicitly mentioned in the Samaritan case, the pattern of events is consistent with the other instances of the Spirit's indwelling. Speaking in tongues can be inferred.[20] Luke's focus on speaking in tongues shows that the phenomenon is an expression of Spirit-inspired speech that miraculously units a diversity of people together in prayer and praise. This pattern is repeated throughout the Acts of the Apostles. Therefore, while speaking in tongues is not mentioned explicitly in the Samaritan case, the Samaritan Spirit baptism brought about unity in prayer and praise to these diverse people, pointing to the presence of speaking in tongues. The wonder of the Samaritans' Spirit baptism for Luke was not in their glossolalic speech but in the fact that a despised group like the Samaritans are commissioned and empowered for the same mission as the Jewish disciples.

Speaking in Tongues for the Church Today

As we have already shown, Luke distinguishes the manifestation of the Holy Spirit that the Samaritans received from the hands of Peter and John as different from their initial faith in Christ. Consequently, it is apparent that the apostles of the early church believed it was a necessity for these believing Samaritans to be baptized in the Holy Spirit. This is demonstrated by the fact that the apostles commissioned Peter and John to travel up to Samaria for the express purpose of seeing the Samaritans baptized in the Holy Spirit. The outward manifestation that the Samaritans received can be logically shown to be speaking in tongues. This leads to an important contemporary question: Is there anything within Luke's account of the Samaritans' Spirit baptism that points to speaking in tongues not being for the church today?

Some cessationists have supposed that, since the Samaritans received the Holy Spirit through the laying on of the apostles' hands, speaking in tongues could only be acquired through the administration of apostolic operation and thereby must have ceased after their departure. Yet, if this had been the divine means for the dispensation of speaking in tongues, then it would seem to follow that the apostles would have received the Holy Spirit at Pentecost first and then laid their hands on the rest of the 120.[21] Additionally, there is no evidence in Scripture that suggests that the Spirit's baptism should only come through some apostolic process. Furthermore,

20. Holdcraft, *Holy Spirit*, 96.

21. Nelson, *Baptism*, 69.

if Spirit baptism is nothing more than a "salvation" experience, then claiming that an apostolic process was required means nobody but the original apostles could receive salvation.

This cessationist position lacks both biblical and historical support. There is no biblical text which requires that Spirit baptism be imparted through the apostolic laying on of hands. While there are certainly instances where God uses this process, to require such a process for Spirit baptism is to add a cessationist pretext to the biblical text. No additional evidence of the inaccuracy of this cessationist point is needed than the fact that Spirit baptism, as evidenced by speaking in tongues, is still widely witnessed today without the use of apostolic administration.

To state that the apostolic means of the Samaritan's receiving the Holy Spirit is evidence for its cessation after the apostolic period is to make a connection that neither Luke nor any of the other New Testament writers intended to make. Simply put, no evidence from this passage points to a cessationist perspective on speaking in tongues. Because of this reality, the obligation to prove the cessation of speaking in tongues from Scripture rests upon the cessationist and not upon the Pentecostal. The clear biblical pattern of Spirit baptism reveals that it should continue throughout the entirety of the church age.

A Lukan theology of Spirit baptism reveals the Spirit's work of breaking down religious and cultural barriers in order to facilitate his missional advancement of the church. Frank Macchia sums it up powerfully by stating:

> Glossolalia in this context is to be seen as an unclassifiable language that points to the hidden mystery of human freedom before God that cuts through differences of gender, class, and culture to reveal a solidarity that is essential to our very being and that is revealed to us in God's own self-disclosure. It is the lowest common denominator between people who might be very different from one another, revealing a deep sense of equality that cannot be denied and that challenges any discrimination based on gender, class, or race.[22]

The work of the Spirit in Samaria is consistent with the unifying portrayal of a Lukan theology of Spirit baptism, which portrays its purpose of missional empowerment and which is not about a salvific experience. Those who receive the Spirit baptism in Luke-Acts are *already* abiding in a right

22. Macchia, "Sighs Too Deep," 66.

16

relationship with God before the occurrence of Spirit baptism. The cessationist perspective fails to consider the context of Scripture accurately; when the context is taken into account, the cessationist argument is refuted. As such, there can be no valid argument for denying that the Samaritan account supports the fact that the ministry of Spirit baptism is still present and relevant for the church today.

In Acts 8, Luke's account of the Samaritans being baptized in the Spirit helps establish a Lukan theology of speaking in tongues as the initial physical evidence of Spirit baptism and empowerment that is relevant to the church today. There is no evidence within Luke's account that would advocate for Philip's gospel message being either incomplete or misunderstood by the Samaritans. That is, the apostles did not go to Samaria to correct or clarify the doctrine of salvation so that regeneration could occur.[23] As such, the sole purpose of the apostles' journey to these believing Samaritans was for them to receive the baptism of the Holy Spirit. And while Luke does not mention glossolalia specifically in this instance, glossolalia can be logically inferred. First, the results of the Samaritans' Spirit baptism are consistent with the day of Pentecost. Second, Simon witnessed something different in these Samaritans that he had never seen before. The one thing that fits these descriptions is speaking in tongues.

THE GENTILE SPIRIT BAPTISM

Acts 10:44–48

> While Peter was still speaking these words, the Holy Spirit fell upon all those who were listening to the message. All the circumcised believers who came with Peter were amazed, because the gift of the Holy Spirit had been poured out on the Gentiles also. For they were hearing them speaking with tongues and exalting God. Then Peter answered, "Surely no one can refuse the water for these to be baptized who have received the Holy Spirit just as we did, can he?" And he ordered them to be baptized in the name of Jesus Christ. Then they asked him to stay on for a few days.

The third passage of Scripture in which Luke mentions speaking in tongues is found in Acts 10:44–48. Luke sets up this account by explaining that the Spirit's work of baptism took place in the midst of a great cultural divide

23. Menzies, *Empowered for Witness*, 208.

that stood between the Jews and Gentiles. No two other people groups had more social, political, and religious barriers than these. However, the Spirit baptism of Cornelius and his household would establish a new precedent for the early church that would enable the fulfillment of Christ's mission (Acts 1:8). Through the divine outpouring of Spirit baptism on these Gentiles, the early church became open to the full inclusion of Gentile believers as coequals under Christ.

Luke identifies the Roman Gentile Cornelius as a God-fearer and a "devout man" (Acts 10:2). Cornelius believed in God, but he could not practice faith in unity with Jewish believers due to cultural barriers. The wonder in Acts 10, then, is not that Gentiles can become believers but that they are admitted as members of the church without the normal process of conversion to Judaism by circumcision first.[24] The most conclusive verification for the apostles that Cornelius and his household could be accepted into the church was the fact that they were baptized in the Holy Spirit, as evidenced by speaking in tongues. Without this external sign, Jewish Christians could debate the validity of the Spirit's work among these Gentiles. However, the unmistakable visible and audible sign of speaking in tongues made what the Spirit had done undeniable to both the apostle Peter and the entire Jewish Christian community. Gentiles had the same Spirit, for their faith in Christ had resulted in the same subsequent work of the Spirit (Acts 10:45–47).

This section makes the case that the manifestation of the Spirit Cornelius experienced continues to support the Lukan theology of speaking in tongues as the initial physical evidence of Spirit baptism. This section will also determine that the passage supports speaking in tongues as a relevant aspect for the church today.

Speaking in Tongues as Initial Physical Evidence

Classical Pentecostals defend speaking in tongues as the initial physical evidence of Spirit baptism by arguing that the historical narrative of Acts should be read both historically and theologically.[25] Luke is not only providing his reader with a historical account of events within the church but also laying out a theological foundation for the church to be built. It is no accident that Luke links the events of Acts 2 to what took place with Cornelius in Acts 10. Luke connects the outpouring of the Spirit at Pentecost to

24. Yong, *Spirit Poured Out*, 84.
25. Keener, *Acts*, 2:1729.

the outpouring of the Spirit given to the Gentile believers. It is evident that for Luke, the phenomenon of speaking in tongues was a sign that validated the baptism of the Holy Spirit.

Not only this, but in examining Luke's narrative, it is clear that speaking in tongues was overwhelming evidence to the other apostles. This one supernatural sign provided all the proof these Jews needed to believe their experience was authentic.[26] It proves that the early church had an inseparable connection between the baptism of the Holy Spirit and speaking in other tongues. Therefore, when we examine the fact that the apostles saw speaking in tongues as the definitive proof that the Gentiles had received the Holy Spirit, we should not be quick to overlook this as supporting evidence for the classical Pentecostal perspective of speaking in tongues as the initial physical evidence of Spirit baptism.

Furthermore, Luke emphasizes speaking in tongues as the initial physical evidence that the Holy Spirit had fallen upon the Gentiles, stating that the Spirit "fell upon *all* those who were listening to the message" (Acts 10:44, italics mine). Not only did these Gentiles experience Spirit baptism as evidenced by tongue speech, but it was the universal nature of speaking in other tongues that became definitive confirmation to the early church that these Gentiles had received the baptism of the Holy Spirit. Luke shows that Peter also identified the universal nature of speaking in other tongues to be consistent with the pattern of Spirit baptism that took place at Pentecost (Acts 10:47). The simple fact remains that Luke wants his audience to understand that speaking in tongues was the vital evidence that affirmed to Jewish believers that the manifestation of the Spirit had also fallen upon the Gentiles.

So strong was this evidence to the early church that even cessationist Watson Mills admits that "there was no valid argument that could be lodged in light of what had happened: the tongues experience was evidence that God's Spirit had overturned Jewish particularism and opened the church to the Gentiles."[27] It was unmistakable that what Cornelius and these Gentile believers received was the same as what the Jews had received on the day of Pentecost. Together, this all aligns with the Pentecostal understanding of speaking in other tongues as the normative evidence of the Holy Spirit's indwelling of a believer.

26. Brumback, *Tongues*, 170.
27. Mills, *Theological/Exegetical Approach*, 71.

The importance of speaking in tongues and its association with Spirit baptism in Acts 10 can also be seen in Luke's describing what these Gentiles received as "the gift of the Holy Spirit" (Acts 2:38; 5:32; 11:17). This characteristically Lukan phrase is also used in Acts 2:38 to refer to the action of the Holy Spirit in baptizing those who have been saved.[28] In distinguishing between repentance that leads to salvific faith and the gift of the Holy Spirit, Robert Menzies points out that "Luke always attributes forgiveness (ἄφεσις), which is granted in response to faith/repentance, to Jesus—never to the Spirit."[29] Thus, to argue that what Cornelius received was only salvation is to ignore Luke's usage of the term "gift of the Spirit." As in Acts 2, Luke is clearly trying to describe something distinct from and subsequent to the work of salvation occurring in the believer's life. The decisive sign of Spirit baptism upon Cornelius and his household (similar to Pentecost) was their reception of the gift of the Holy Spirit through the visible sign of their speaking in tongues. Without the physical evidence of Spirit-inspired tongue speech, the Jewish and Gentile unification into the church would not have happened either as quickly or as peacefully as it did. But having witnessed these Gentiles speaking in tongues—if it was a sign of Spirit baptism—there could be no argument made for not accepting them as part of the Jesus community.

It is also essential to consider that when Peter retells the supernatural events that took place to those in Jerusalem, he believes that speaking in tongues is such a normative pattern that he proclaims, "The Holy Spirit fell upon them just as He did upon us at the beginning" (Acts 11:15). Therefore, by the witness of the apostles and the testimony of their experience with Cornelius and his household, it is evident that what occurred through their speaking in other tongues should be seen as the same baptism of the Holy Spirit that indwelt the apostles on the day of Pentecost. Moreover, if those present were persuaded that what the Gentiles had received was an equivalent Holy Spirit experience, then speaking in tongues must be the unmistakable initial evidence of Holy Spirit baptism.

Some have backed away from supporting speaking in tongues as initial physical evidence of Spirit baptism out of fear that such a position creates a division of Christian "classes." However, Spirit baptism is not about making those who speak in tongues "better" than Christians who have never spoken in tongues. Spirit baptism does not make one more saved or "better" than

28. Ervin, *Spirit Baptism*, 78.
29. Menzies, *Empowered for Witness*, 217.

the one who is not Spirit baptized. Instead, the emphasis is not compara-tive—the one who is Spirit baptized versus the one who is not—but rather the point is that Spirit baptism makes the one who is baptized "better" by missionally equipping them with "power from on high" (Luke 24:49; Acts 1:8). In other words, initial physical evidence of Spirit baptism does not create a problem of classification of Christians, but as pictured in the Acts of the Apostles, speaking in tongues empowers the church to be united in mission and equipped for service.

Speaking in Tongues for the Church Today

Since Luke is clear that it was through the baptism of the Holy Spirit—evidenced by speaking in tongues—that the apostles accepted Gentiles as believers, some cessationists have argued that this was the primary pur-pose of speaking in tongues. And since that "revelation" has been fulfilled, speaking in tongues no longer has any relevance for the church today. As one such cessationist writes, "Since the purpose of tongues in Acts 10 was to authenticate a new revelation to the early church, and since the biblical significance and theological implications of this new revelation have been inscripturated, it is apparent then that the gift has served its purpose."[30] Yet, if this were true, it would seem to follow that the account of Cornelius and his household would have been the last time in Scripture where we see the practice of speaking in tongues in association with Spirit baptism. But the events of Acts 10 do not conclude the New Testament account of speaking in tongues, nor do they even complete Luke's reports of speaking in tongues as part of the baptism of the Holy Spirit. Instead, the events of Acts 10 reveal a consistent pattern in Luke's narrative in which he portrays the con-tinual working of Spirit baptism that is evidenced by speaking in tongues.

Having witnessed Cornelius and his household's glossolalic baptism in the Holy Spirit, Peter is quick to affirm their status as members of the church, removing any doubt as to the validity of what they had received. Peter says, "Surely no one can refuse the water for these to be baptized who have received the Holy Spirit *just as we did*, can he?" (Acts 10:47, italics mine). The evidence of glossolalia proved to be the distinguishing feature which revealed to the early church that these Gentiles were already a part of the church. Stanley Horton states, "Peter recognized this as further con-firmation that these Gentiles believers were not only accepted by God but

30. Marbell, "Speaking in Tongues," 63.

were made part of the church."[31] Throughout his narrative, Luke highlights the fundamental fact that baptism in the Holy Spirit is for all peoples, in all ages.

Affirming this point, John Wyckoff writes, "Pentecostals believe that the distinctive experience of the baptism of the Holy Spirit, such as Luke describes, is crucial to the contemporary church."[32] Historically, Pentecostals have argued that baptism in the Spirit is a separate experience from conversion. Even when it is granted that Spirit baptism and regeneration can coincide, Pentecostals preserve a logical distinction of progression of both experiences.[33] Therefore, just as Luke, writing under the inspiration of the Spirit, depicts the baptism of the Holy Spirit being intended for all believers, Pentecostals maintain that this biblical pattern still applies to the church today. Suppose the early church believed and accepted that speaking in tongues could be for all believers. In that case, it follows that the biblical pattern set forth by the early church was of a continuation of Holy Spirit baptism as evidenced by speaking in tongues and not the cessation of Spirit baptism. The connection between Acts 2:4 and 10:46 implies that tongues played a significant role universally in the early church; Luke's account of the baptism of the Holy Spirit being poured out upon Cornelius and his household continues the consistent pattern for the Lukan theology of speaking in tongues. This account supports the function and purpose of speaking in tongues as the initial physical evidence of Holy Spirit baptism, a baptism extended for the Gentiles. As followers of God, these Gentiles' faith was confirmed to the Jewish community of Christ followers through the fact that upon receiving Spirit baptism, they spoke in other tongues (Acts 10:45–47).

Additionally, this account of speaking in tongues provides support for the relevancy of glossolalic activity for the church today by serving as a unifying agent within the early church. As the means of uniting the Jews and Gentiles, Spirit baptism was instrumental in revealing that all people can become a part of the church. As such, it can be logically concluded that the Lukan theology of speaking in tongues includes the phenomenon as a critical, active, aspect of the church which is not meant to be discontinued.

31. Horton, *Book of Acts*, 135.

32. Wyckoff, "Baptism," 448.

33. Vondey, *Pentecostal Theology*, 94.

PAUL AND THE EPHESIAN DISCIPLES

Acts 19:1–7

> It happened that while Apollos was at Corinth, Paul passed through the upper country and came to Ephesus, and found some disciples. He said to them, "Did you receive the Holy Spirit when you believed?" And they said to him, "No, we have not even heard whether there is a Holy Spirit." And he said, "Into what then were you baptized?" And they said, "Into John's baptism." Paul said, "John baptized with the baptism of repentance, telling the people to believe in Him who was coming after him, that is, in Jesus." When they heard this, they were baptized in the name of the Lord Jesus. And when Paul had laid his hands upon them, the Holy Spirit came on them, and they began speaking with tongues and prophesying. There were in all about twelve men.

The fourth and final occurrence of speaking in tongues in Luke's account of the early church takes place among some disciples of John the Baptist living in Ephesus. Because this account also includes the apostle Paul, it provides us with a unifying understanding of Lukan and Pauline theology concerning the purpose and function of speaking in tongues. These events occurred near the end of Paul's missionary ministry, over twenty years after the original outpouring of the Spirit at Pentecost.[34] The fact that these events take place over two decades after Pentecost suggests that Spirit baptism was never intended to be only for the "first" generation of Christ followers. Instead, Spirit baptism according to a Lukan theology supports a continuationist perspective of their operation within the church today.

Luke records that Paul inquires about the pneumatological experience of these Ephesian disciples and quickly learns that they are unaware of the Holy Spirit's arrival. However, Luke describes these Ephesians as both disciples and believers, clearly indicating that they understood salvation through repentance (Acts 19:4). But through Paul's words, they now responded in salvific faith to Christ and were baptized (Acts 19:5). The sequence of events described by Luke shows that these Ephesian believers received the baptism of the Holy Spirit *after* they had received saving faith. If the Holy Spirit's regeneration work was all they could receive, then Paul should have been satisfied once they believed and were baptized in water. However, it is clear that Paul was not content until these new Christians

34. Holdcraft, *Holy Spirit*, 97.

received the baptism of the Holy Spirit.[35] Without question, the apostle Paul understood that the means of salvation is not appropriated through the laying on of hands (Rom 8). Therefore, by laying his hands on the Ephesians, the purpose was not salvific but for what immediately transpired— the baptism of the Holy Spirit.

Thus, without question, these Ephesian believers were regenerated prior to their baptism in water, and their glossolalic Spirit baptism was subsequent to their salvific faith. In Acts 19, Luke emphasizes the fact that Paul did not lay his hands on these Ephesians to receive the Holy Spirit until he was confident of their faith in Christ.

Speaking in Tongues as Initial Physical Evidence

Just as with the other Lukan accounts of Spirit baptism, the external, visible proof that the Ephesians had been baptized in the Holy Spirit was that they spoke in other tongues. The pattern of Lukan theology of speaking in tongues is repeated within the Ephesian Pentecost because when the Holy Spirit came upon them as part of Spirit baptism, they began to speak in tongues and prophesy (Acts 19:6).

The above notwithstanding, some theologians have argued that Luke's recording of these disciples speaking in other tongues upon receiving the Holy Spirit does not imply that tongues must accompany Spirit reception in every individual instance.[36] This argument is based solely on the Samaritan case in Acts 8, for in all other instances of Holy Spirit baptism, the manifestation of speaking in tongues is clearly stated (Acts 2, 10, 19). Furthermore, while Acts 8 does not explicitly state that those who received the Holy Spirit spoke in tongues, the narrative strongly points to the presence of speaking in tongues; thus, any objective reader can logically infer its existence. To dismiss the evidence of speaking in tongues accompanying Spirit baptism in each of the other accounts because it is not explicitly stated in one is to err on the side of the exception rather than the distinct biblical pattern that Luke sets forth.

Cessationist Watson Mills argues that the speaking in tongues at Ephesus was simply Luke's way of showing that God's approval rested upon the experience of these people, and that it was not Luke's intention that subsequent generations of Christians formalize the events into a religious

35. Linzey, *Baptism*, 104.
36. Keener, *Acts*, 3:2823.

directive that was superior to any other manifestation of Spirit possession.[37] However, to minimize Spirit baptism to simply "God's approval" is to mischaracterize Luke's explicit portrayal of the purpose and function of speaking in tongues. The repeated evidence of those who received the baptism of the Holy Spirit is that they spoke in other tongues. As such, the Pentecostal understanding of speaking in tongues as the initial physical evidence of Spirit baptism is consistent with the Lukan description of its arrival.

Interpreting Luke's connection between Spirit baptism and speaking in tongues fairly recognizes that the latter was not an occasional option; but a reoccurring, definitive pattern that the Holy Spirit established.[38] Speaking in tongues is not presented as evidence of Spirit baptism randomly, but rather it is the supernatural connection between human recipients and Spirit empowerment. At its core, speaking in tongues encompasses an encounter with a divine person whose purpose for sending the Spirit is to transform humanity into his missional partners in advancing God's kingdom (Acts 1:8). The classical Pentecostal position that speaking in tongues serves as the initial physical evidence of Spirit baptism is not so much a sign that we are in possession of the Spirit but that the Spirit is in possession of us.[39] Having submitted to Spirit-inspired speech, supernatural empowerment for witness flows naturally from this human-divine phenomenon. As such, the Pentecostal views evidential tongues not as the "goal" of seeking Spirit baptism but merely as the sign that supernatural empowerment has occurred. The "goal" of Spirit baptism is that the life of the believer would be empowered for witness by being "clothed with power from on high" (Luke 24:29).

Furthermore, the classical Pentecostal sees a vital connection between the evidential-tongues doctrine and the widespread supernatural manifestations that brought about the tremendous growth of Pentecostalism throughout its history. Having read Luke's accounts of Spirit baptism in the Acts of the Apostles, Pentecostals have sought the same power and experience that marked the early church. Through this unique reading of Acts, Pentecostals have maintained an expectation of Spirit empowerment, resulting in a dramatic shift within Christendom. The fact that the modern Pentecostal movement became an exploding missionary movement marked by miraculous signs should not be considered a mere coincidence. Classical

37. Mills, *Theological/Exegetical Approach*, 73.

38. Holdcroft, *Holy Spirit*, 105.

39. Macchia, "Question of Tongues," 121.

Pentecostals maintain that Luke does not present evidential tongues merely as an arbitrary sign but as centrally connected to the missional purpose of Spirit baptism.

Speaking in Tongues for the Church Today

Within this final Lukan account of speaking in tongues, a biblical framework for understanding the purpose and function of speaking in tongues as the initial physical evidence of Spirit baptism has been presented. Furthermore, since Spirit baptism aims to aid in the missional work of the church, it is logical to conclude that Spirit baptism (and by necessity, speaking in tongues) is just as essential for the church today as it was in its infancy.

When the apostle Paul layed his hands on these twelve Ephesian disciples, they were immediately baptized in the Holy Spirit and began to speak in other tongues. Thus, speaking in tongues should not be viewed as an arbitrary sign; it signifies the Spirit's fullness and empowerment for a universal mission. Speaking in tongues is inseparable from the church's foundational assignment.[40] Yet, some have tried to cast doubt on the unified nature of Luke's accounts of speaking in tongues. Frank Beare attempts to negate the importance of speaking in tongues in connection with Spirit baptism with the following words:

> It is sufficient to note that glossolalia is not regarded by any New Testament author as a normal or invariable accompaniment of the life of grace, and there is no justification in the classical documents of the Christian faith for holding it to be a necessary element in the fullest spiritual development of the individual Christian or in the corporate life of the church.[41]

However, if it was *not* Luke's intention to show speaking in tongues as the vital connector to Spirit baptism and to associate it with the church's call to missional engagement, then Luke was unsuccessful in depicting the cause of the first-century church's empowerment. Instead, a biblically based Lukan theology of speaking in tongues provides us with a connection between Spirit baptism and Spirit empowerment, which offers us a foundation for understanding the church's exciting and diverse charismatic structure.

---

40. Keener, "Spirit's Empowerment," 183.
41. Bear, "Speaking with Tongues," 231.

The work of the Holy Spirit is a central theme within Luke's accounts. Coupled with how Luke clearly outlines the Spirit's movements, it is unmistakable that a proper Lukan theology of Spirit baptism is that it is for those who have already experienced the regenerative work of the Spirit. Therefore, as the repeated signifier of Spirit baptism, a Lukan theology of speaking in tongues presents the phenomenon as the unique indicator that a person has received supernatural empowerment for service and mission. In addition, a Lukan theology of speaking in tongues reveals the precise pattern of its necessity throughout various times and people groups. As such, it is reasonable to assert that speaking in tongues should not be limited to a particular generation or people group but should continue throughout the entirety of the church age.

Some, even within Pentecostalism, would like to move away from connecting speaking in tongues as the initial sign of Spirit baptism. This shift from traditional Pentecostal doctrine hinges on the belief that while tongues may serve as "one" sign of Spirit baptism, it should not be viewed as *the* exclusive sign. The case for this position rests upon the fact that there is no explicit teaching within the New Testament that requires speaking in tongues as the sign of Spirit baptism. However, the lack of a biblical imperative that explicitly commands Spirit baptism to be evidenced by speaking in tongues does nothing to negate the clear Lukan pattern established within the Acts of the Apostles. To throw out the testimony of Luke's accounts of Spirit baptism—which are evidenced by speaking in tongues—simply because the rest of the New Testament does not lay out a systematic theology of the doctrine does nothing to invalidity the clear testimony of Luke's record of Spirit baptism within the early church. To declare a doctrine invalid simply because the New Testament writers do not offer an explicit, systematic defense of the doctrine is an inappropriate approach to scriptural truth. For example, the doctrine of the Trinity is nowhere explicitly laid out by the New Testament writers in any systematic way. However, this fact should not cause us to doubt the clear biblical revelation of the Godhead existing as one essence made up of three distinct persons.

When looked at objectively, the problem is not that Luke was unclear with his writings on speaking in tongues, but rather that it is the presupposition on the part of those who would like to marginalize its value for the church today. Stronstad writes on the charismatic Lukan theology that can be found in the New Testament:

To interpret Luke's charismatic theology as dispensational, abnormal, and secondary, however, reveals more about the attitudes of contemporary interpreters and the theological and ecclesiastical traditions they are defending than it does about the activity of the Holy Spirit in Luke-Acts. The witness of the Gospel of Luke is that by the empowering of the Holy Spirit Jesus was a charismatic. Similarly, the witness of the Acts of the Apostles is that the disciples were a charismatic community. Thus, in the theology of Luke the church is charismatic.[42]

A careful investigation of Luke's accounts of speaking in tongues leads to only one conclusion. Speaking in tongues is meant to be an active part of the orthodox Christian faith. The evidence points to it functioning both as the initial physical evidence of Holy Spirit baptism and as a source of empowerment for ministry purposes to continue through all generations of the church. The evidence is substantial and is based upon the complete scriptural narrative of Luke's writings, and it offers a logical determination for a Lukan theology of speaking in tongues.

CONCLUSION

The four occurrences of speaking in tongues in Luke's account of the Acts of the Apostles reveal a thoroughly charismatic community of believers who experienced and accepted speaking in tongues as accompanying Spirit baptism. Because Luke appears to center his entire narrative around charismatic workings within the early church, it is no surprise that he records the presence of speaking in tongues from the beginning (Acts 2) to the end (Acts 19) of his account. No other New Testament writer emphasizes the visible work of the Spirit as much as Luke does in his Acts of the Apostles. It is evident that Luke intends to depict the Spirit's empowerment of the church as including the external evidence of miracles, prophecies, healings, and speaking in other tongues.

Significantly, a Lukan theology of speaking in tongues reveals that this charismatic work of the Spirit is separate from the initial salvific work of the Spirit. This subsequent work of the Spirit shows that Luke believes that the purifying work of the Spirit (salvation) is not equivalent to his empowering work (Spirit baptism). A classical Pentecostal perspective of Spirit baptism recognizes the importance of the Spirit being practically "evidenced" in this

42. Stronstad, *Charismatic Theology*, 97.

present world. While some within Christendom have sought to make the working of the Spirit a mysterious force that is detached from any discernable experience, the Pentecostal pushes back against such ideas by pointing to a Lukan theology of the Spirit which testifies to the evidential nature of the Spirit's work in the lives of believers.

2

A Pauline Theology
of Speaking in Tongues

BRIDGING LUKAN AND PAULINE THEOLOGIES

WHILE LUKE NARRATES THE Holy Spirit's role within the early church, the apostle Paul writes from a teaching perspective by writing to various churches that he has planted concerning the person and nature of the Spirit. The variance in writing style (narrative for Luke verses letters for Paul) has led some to question whether or not a unifying methodology of their beliefs concerning speaking in tongues can be achieved. However, it should be pointed out that achieving a biblically accurate position on any doctrine requires the integration of numerous authors using a variety of methodological approaches. That is to say, it should be expected that developing a biblical framework of speaking in tongues would require a unifying of theological perspectives from within the biblical canon. A Lukan theology of speaking in tongues focuses on its functioning as the initial physical evidence of Spirit baptism and its being relevant for the church today. A Pauline theology of speaking in tongues builds upon this Lukan theology by examining its theological and practical operation within the church.

Within Luke's final account of speaking in tongues (Acts 19), three key factors provide an essential link between a Lukan and a Pauline theology of speaking in tongues. Firstly, there is the apparent logistical correlation. The apostle Paul was present in Luke's final account of speaking in tongues. The significance of this connection cannot be underestimated. The fact that Paul plays a vital role within the narrative of the Ephesian disciples receiving the baptism of the Holy Spirit creates a critical bridge between Paul's practical experience with speaking in tongues and his writings concerning the subject. Secondly, there is a historical connection between the events in Acts 19 and Paul's writings to the Corinthian church. After planting the Corinthian church (Acts 18), Paul traveled to Ephesus, where he taught for two years in the lecture hall of Tyrannus (Acts 19:8–10). Therefore, it is probable that Paul wrote to the church at Corinth in AD 55 or 56 while residing in Ephesus.[1] This connection implies that Paul's communication with the Corinthian church took place in close proximity to the glossolalic experience of the Ephesian disciples that Luke records in Acts 19. Finally, there are solid theological connections between Luke's final account of speaking in tongues and Paul's writings to the Corinthians. Stanley Horton says:

> The parallels between Acts and 1 Corinthians 14 indicate that the gift is the same in form as the evidence of Acts; however, the purpose of tongues in 1 Corinthians 12 is a gift used in the church and needing interpretation to bring edification.[2]

Therefore, through the logistical, historical, and theological connections found in Luke's narrative of the Ephesian disciples' Spirit baptism, a unified theological perspective of speaking in tongues emerges between a Lukan and a Pauline theology of the phenomenon. While a Lukan and a Pauline theology of speaking in tongues may focus on different aspects of its function, they are united in their understanding of its essential nature as an indication of Spirit baptism.

Paul does not focus on speaking in tongues as the initial physical evidence of Spirit baptism in his Letter to the Corinthians. At the same time, Luke, through his narrative account, provides evidence for this association. Still, Paul does build upon the idea that speaking in tongues is a means for the church to receive missional empowerment through its use of spiritual manifestations. It is clear, then, that in addition to the salvific functions of a Pauline pneumatology, there is a charismatic endowment and gifting featured prominently in a Pauline theology of the Spirit.[3] Because of this, the theological importance of Paul's Letter to the Corinthians cannot be overlooked in establishing the proper function of the Spirit in the church today. Gordon Fee explains this in his commentary:

1. Hamar, *Book of First Corinthians*, 13.
2. Horton, *What the Bible Says*, 223.
3. Kärkkäinen, *Pneumatology*, 19.

Perhaps the single greatest theological contribution of our letter to the Christian faith is Paul's understanding of the nature of the church, especially in its local expression. If the gospel itself is at stake in the Corinthians' theology and behavior, so also is its visible expression in the local community of redeemed people. The net result is more teaching on the church here than in any of Paul's letters.[4]

Paul's Letter to the Corinthians, then, serves as a significant theological source for how the modern church should conduct itself. Through this epistle, Paul teaches how the church should function under various circumstances, and one of those subjects is the appropriate function of speaking in tongues within the church.

Some cessationists have suggested that it is impossible to develop a Pauline theological doctrine of speaking in tongues based on a historical-critical view of the text. They argue that since Paul's epistles were designed for a particular people, it is inappropriate to draw practical theology from these texts bound within a specific set of circumstances. Victor Furnish takes a stand in favor of this position:

> The practical significance of this letter for the church today has become increasingly problematic. For example, there can be no disputing that Paul's counsels to the Corinthians about matters of sex, eating meat from pagan temples, and employment of spiritual gifts presupposed social conditions and a congregational situation quite specific to his time and a particular place. It is, therefore, a serious misappropriation of the letter whenever its counsels are enjoined uncritically on Christians today, who are confronted, both individually and corporately, with social and political realities that are in most cases very different from those in Roman Corinth.[5]

Without question, a historical-critical approach is helpful in understanding the occasion for Paul's epistle and the conditions within Rome and the Corinthian church at the time of his writing. However, these details do not prohibit the modern church from applying the truths within this epistle to our current age. In fact, many of the problems within the Corinthian church can be summarized as either asceticism or hedonism philosophy, which are still widely present within the modern church. Furthermore,

---

4. Fee, *First Epistle*, 19.
5. Furnish, *New Testament Theology*, 143.

since every biblical writer is "bound" to write within their time period, within their cultural problems, and within their geographical constraints, obfuscating their writings on this premise necessitates the dismissal of the entire biblical canon.[6]

While most Christians today do not deal with the situation of meat sacrificed to idols, there are similar issues in which Paul's theological principles can be applied in every culture and time period. Additionally, Paul's principles and applications regarding immoral sexual practices in 1 Corinthians continue to be relevant within the contemporary church. Similarly, Paul's discourse regarding the use of spiritual manifestations should be viewed as relevant for the church today.

In examining Lukan and Pauline theologies concerning speaking in tongues, cessationists have advocated that there are irreconcilable theological differences between their views on the subject. However, if Paul viewed the Corinthians' speaking in tongues as somehow deficient or different from the speaking in tongues that was administered by his own hands upon the Ephesian disciples in Acts 19, then the Corinthian incident would have been an opportune time to rebuke its use. Instead, Paul clearly embraces the use of speaking in tongues within the church as a whole and does not correct the Corinthian theological understanding of speaking in tongues other than to address their mishandling of its practice within the local assembly.

Within this introduction, the phenomenon of speaking in tongues has been shown to have logical, geographical, and theological connections between the writings of Luke and the apostle Paul. These connections further support the continuity and continuation of speaking in tongues. In addition, given Paul's concern for the appropriate usage of speaking in tongues within the Corinthian church, it is evident that speaking in tongues should continue within the church today. With this foundation, the remainder of this chapter will address four frameworks for understanding the proper function of speaking in tongues laid out by Paul in 1 Cor 12–14.

FRAMEWORK #1—DIVERSITY WITHIN UNITY

The overarching purpose of Paul's Letter to the Corinthians is to correct the non-Christian behavior that had manifested itself within the church. Of the apparent problems rampant in the Corinthian congregation, one that was

---

6. For an analysis of historical criticism, see Stuhlmacher, *Historical Criticism*.

of special importance to Paul was the issue of division.[7] Examples of Paul's rebuking of the Corinthians for not seeking unity can be found throughout the letter (1 Cor 1:10–13; 3:3–4; 10:16–17; 11:18). Given this overarching theme, it makes sense that Paul would emphasize the importance of unity within spiritual manifestations in the latter portion of the letter. To this point, Paul explains that the proper function of the Spirit's manifestation within the church derives from a dualistic nature of diversity within unity.

In order to develop this idea, Paul provides two examples. First, he puts forward the diversity within the unity of Christ's body, and then he illustrates the diversity within the unity of spiritual manifestations (1 Cor 12:4–26). From the outset of the discussion of the Spirit's manifestations, Paul seeks to frame the conversation within the theological context of diversity within unity. Macchia sums up the significance of this connection:

> The unity of the persons of the Trinity is not found in some abstract divine substance, nor in an absolute divine subject, since this would subordinate and even dissolve the differences among the divine persons. The persons in relation constitute both their differences and their unity. The ancient concept *perichoresis* (mutual indwelling) is used to explain the divine life shared by Father, Son, and Spirit.[8]

There can be little doubt that Paul's introduction to spiritual gifts is intended to connect the diversity of gifts, services, and workings in the context of the unity between the same Spirit, Lord, and God (1 Cor 12:4–6). Just as the Trinity consists of a unified essence but also a diversity in personhood, all spiritual manifestations derive from the same source (the Spirit) but have various ways in which they are designed to function. Therefore, it is Paul's plain intention that his reader catch the implications of diversity within unity as an essential framework for understanding spiritual manifestations.

In light of this reality, Paul's introductory statement provides a critical theological lens for comprehending the Spirit's ability to be present among his people within a variety of manifestations. To this point, Gordon Fee writes:

> These opening sentences seem intended to give the theological context within which all that follows is to be understood. Each begins with different kinds of manifestations, making clear where

7. Johnson, *1 Corinthians*, 23.

8. Macchia, *Baptized in the Spirit*, 120.

Paul's emphasis lies, and each is followed by a noun that characterizes the activity of one person of the Trinity."[9]

Paul's clear Trinitarian expression of the divine fellowship of diversity within unity influences his understanding of how the church should operate.
This gives credit to the charismatic view of the church, which emphasizes
the importance of fellowship (κοινωνία) within the context of the diversity
of unity.

The argument for Paul within this framework shatters typical societal
traditions for valuing individual members (1 Cor 12:22–24). For Paul, there
is a natural correlation between the divine principle of diversity within
unity and the mutual equality of each diverse individual within the local
assembly. In fact, he argues that those members who would "seem" to be
less honorable or respected are instead supposed to be shown greater honor
and respect. Rather than denigrating some spiritual manifestations within
the body, Paul calls for the acceptance of all spiritual manifestations based
on their intrinsic value to the whole. While there may be debate over the
exact number and distinctions of spiritual manifestations, it seems evident
that Paul viewed charisma as operating within a wide range of functions.

The underlying motivation for accepting all the manifestations of the
Spirit within the church is to prevent division within a church that is designed to be unified together in Christ (1 Cor 12:24–27). Fee sums up this
point eloquently:

> The body is one, yet the body has many parts. In saying that it is
> one, his concern is for its essential unity. But that does not mean
> uniformity. That was the Corinthian error, to think that uniformity
> was a value, or that it represented true spirituality. Paul's concern
> is for their unity; but for him, there is no such thing as true unity
> without diversity.[10]

To provide a practical example of the Spirit's work of diversity within unity
inside the local church, Paul outlines a sizeable list of ways in which the
manifestation of the Spirit is evident (1 Cor 12:7–10). Through careful examination of this list, it is clear that these manifestations are all intended
to be *visible* manifestations of the Spirit's presence working within the
church. The truly remarkable nature of these manifestations is not their
individual uniqueness but the fact that they are *all* observable supernatural

9. Fee, *First Epistle*, 650.

10. Fee, *God's Empowering Presence*, 178.

manifestations of the Spirit within the church. With this understanding, Paul unmistakably identifies speaking in tongues as a valid and valued manifestation of the Spirit within the church.

Since Paul identifies speaking in tongues as an appropriate spiritual manifestation that could operate within the Corinthian church, the Pentecostal is right to emphasize the importance of speaking in tongues as part of the diverse work of the Spirit in our present day. The fact that there is a wide diversity of spiritual manifestations laid out by Paul can be seen to be consistent with the diverse way in which the Spirit has chosen to work throughout Scripture. Just as the Spirit empowered different people in various ways within the Old Testament, it should not be surprising that the Spirit working in the New Testament is characterized by a diversity of manifestations. In this way, the Pentecostal perspective of spiritual manifestations causes Pentecostals to be more open to the work of the Spirit, for they inherently recognize the fact that the Spirit works from a framework of diversity within unity. In other words, it is the belief in a diversity of spiritual manifestations that allows Pentecostals to be welcoming to the Spirit's work being facilitated in various manners. Just as the Pentecostal can be confident in the Spirit's working within the church through a variety of spiritual manifestations, so also can the Pentecostal be confident in the Spirit's ability to work through the church in a variety of methods. Given this reality, it is understandable that Pentecostalism views speaking in tongues as the critical contributor to their radical openness to the Spirit's work in the church today.

The fact that spiritual manifestations are designed to work within the framework of diversity within unity means that we reflect the unity and diversity of both the Godhead and the church. In displaying the variety of spiritual manifestations within unity, a visible reflection of the invisible is accomplished. This connection was indeed not lost to Paul, who intentionally illustrates the unity within the diversity of spiritual manifestations with the unity within diversity of both the Trinity and the church (1 Cor 12:4–6; 12–14). The fact that Paul links spiritual manifestations with the Godhead and the church supports the Pentecostal continuist perspective on spiritual manifestations.

Paul's emphasis on spiritual manifestations working in connection with diversity within unity clearly includes the function of speaking in tongues within the church. A healthy, Spirit-empowered church makes room for speaking in tongues within its expression of spiritual manifestations. This is accomplished by valuing all spiritual manifestations and recognizing their united function within the Spirit for empowering the church. For Paul, the central concern in 1 Cor 12–14 is not the elimination of speaking in tongues within the local assembly but rather its proper function. This is why, in concluding his comments, Paul warns the Corinthians not to hinder people from speaking in other tongues (1 Cor 14:39). Instead, a Pauline theology of the proper function of spiritual manifestations within the church includes the endorsement of speaking in tongues as part of a diverse unity within the church (1 Cor 14:18). From this foundational framework, Paul will next build a case for the proper use of speaking in tongues within the church to ensure that the practice of tongue speech is mutually beneficial to the entire body.

FRAMEWORK #2—ORDER FOR EDIFICATION

A careful examination of 1 Cor 12–14 shows that Paul's central concern regarding speaking in tongues (as with all spiritual manifestations) is that it operate in an orderly manner within the church. If it does not, the entire assembly may misinterpret the Spirit's movement. Thus, Paul's instructions regarding speaking in tongues revolve around the central idea that they must function in an orderly manner to ensure that the church receives true and proper edification.

It is important to note that the term "edification" in 1 Corinthians is taken from the act of building a physical structure. This concept is also consistent with Paul's emphasis elsewhere on being "built up" into the fullness of Christ through the assistance of all the saints (Eph 4:12–13). Paul believed that all the manifestations of the Spirit were given to the church for the benefit and building up of the whole body (1 Cor 12:7), and as Spirit-inspired utterances, speaking in tongues (when interpreted) falls under this category.

Within the context of 1 Cor 12–14, it is clear that Paul's primary focus is *not* the self-edification of the private devotional lives of the individual Corinthian members. Instead, his focus is on the edification of the corporate worship service, the assembly of God's people. Speaking in tongues done within a corporate setting which only edifies the speaker and not the church goes beyond its intended purpose. Paul requires speaking in tongues within a corporate assembly to be interpreted because, by definition, speaking in tongues is unintelligible language. If speaking in tongues is in an incomprehensible language, then if practiced within a corporate setting without interpretation, the church cannot understand what is said; thus, the practice cannot be edifying.[11] With this in mind, it is understandable that Paul views the entire assembly's mutual benefit as an essential requisite of the proper functioning of spiritual manifestations.[12] It is precisely this safeguard that Paul is warning the Corinthian church not to violate. When it comes to speaking in tongues, Paul further explains that this safeguard of the edification of the entire body can only be achieved through the interpretation of tongues (1 Cor 14:5).

Speaking in tongues, as unintelligible speech to both the speaker (1 Cor 14:14) and to those who hear it (14:16), is incapable of being edifying within a corporate setting unless it is interpreted. Given this, Paul's instruction is that speaking in tongues be interpreted in the assembly so that this spiritual manifestation can edify the whole congregation. Paul illustrates the importance of interpretation in association with public speaking in tongues by offering three analogies: musical instruments, a battle call, and foreign languages (1 Cor 14:6–11). Essentially, Paul is arguing that if the noise coming from the instrument makes no sense, it has no benefit to the hearer. Likewise, in the example of foreign languages, if the hearer does not understand the language, it is of no value.

Paul's practical illustrations provide the logical foundation for why speaking in tongues needs to be interpreted within the community of worshipers.[13] Since speaking in tongues does not possess cognitive communicative properties between humans, Paul's analogies leave no occasion for doubt concerning the necessity of interpretation when believers are gathered in corporate worship. Additionally, it should be noted that the Corinthian custom of uninterpreted tongues within the local assembly was Paul's central concern, *not* speaking in tongues per se. To this point, Paul clearly expresses his desire that they would all speak in tongues (1 Cor 14:5). The problem for Paul is not speaking in tongues but rather its non-interpreted use within the Corinthian church, which renders the spiritual manifestation useless and causes the assembly not to be edified.

Speaking in tongues done outside of the corporate worship service needs no interpretation because the communication is done directly to the Spirit from within the practitioner's spirit. The direct, Spirit-inspired

11. Fee, *First Epistle*, 727.
12. Holdcraft, *Holy Spirit*, 179.
13. Fee, *God's Empowering Presence*, 226.

communication done within a private setting is interpreted by the Spirit, who understands our "groanings that cannot be uttered" (Rom 8:26). Paul's own testimony of his intimate practice of speaking in tongues reveals his support of its practice within a private setting. While Paul speaks very favorably about speaking in tongues within the context of personal prayer and praise, however, he adamantly warns about speaking in tongues in public unless interpreted (1 Cor 14:5, 13, 27). This difference can be understood by viewing speaking in tongues through Paul's framework of the priority of edification within the worship assembly. If no one interprets the spiritual manifestation of speaking in tongues, confusion is created among the assembly. However, once speaking in tongues is interpreted, it no longer remains unintelligible speech but becomes an intelligible utterance that satisfies the necessity of spiritual manifestations being edifying to the entire congregation.

FRAMEWORK #3 — PRAYER AND PRAISE TO GOD

Paul's priority of edification in the use of spiritual manifestations explains the proper function of speaking in tongues within the church. Still, it does not explain the exact nature of speaking in tongues as a spiritual manifestation. His words in Corinthians clarify that he believed the function of speaking in tongues to be prayer and praise to God (1 Cor 14:13–19). For Paul, the activity of speaking in tongues as a means of prayer and praise was not merely a theoretical supposition but an active knowing from personal experience (1 Cor 14:14, 15, 18). From this intimate knowledge of speaking in tongues, he concluded the phenomenon to be the product of Spirit-directed activity within the practitioner's life. As a result of this practical knowledge, he describes speaking in tongues as prayer and praise focused on God in the language of Spirit inspiration.[14]

Paul explains that when praying and praising through speaking in tongues, the human mind is "unfruitful." Because of this, some cessationist have suggested that the act of speaking in tongues is, therefore, unproductive. However, this is clearly not Paul's intention, for it is logically incoherent for Paul to confess his practice of glossolalic speech while simultaneously teaching that its practice has no value. Instead, Paul is merely pointing out that speaking in tongues cannot be understood by either the speaker or the listener. Since by definition speaking in tongues is unintelligible language,

14. Fee, *First Epistle*, 742.

the term "unfruitful" refers to the non-semantic nature of the practice. Paul's objective here is to differentiate between praying in tongues, which is not understood, and prayer and praise that are done in a known language.[15] In making this distinction, Paul does nothing to minimize the role of speaking in tongues as personal prayer and praise. Instead, Paul affirms both prayer and praise that originate as part of speaking in tongues and prayer and praise in known languages (1 Cor 14:15).

All prayer and praise to God must embody the Spirit. Therefore, prayer and praise done without understanding (speaking in tongues) is not more "spiritual" than prayer and praise done with understanding. Instead, the distinction is in the different modes of prayer and praise, not in the "spiritual" nature of either kind. Both have their respective benefits. To this point, Paul explains that he freely participates in both modes (1 Cor 14:15) and seems to have no problem with the fact that one mode of prayer and praise (speaking in tongues) does not benefit his understanding. Therefore, to deny a biblically supported mode of prayer and praise (speaking in tongues), as the cessationists attempt to do, is to reject an essential means of communicating with God. The power of speaking in tongues can be found in the fact that it enables divine communication to go beyond the limits of human communication (Rom 8:26).

Since the nature of speaking in tongues is fundamentally prayer and praise, it should function similarly in both the personal and the corporate settings. The main distinction lies in the need for interpretation within the corporate assembly, while there is no need for an interpretation if done privately. (1 Cor 14:16). Although one mode (with knowledge) is clearly for the benefit of others and the second mode (without knowledge) is done for the benefit of the individual person, Paul holds both as legitimate means for believers to operate in the Spirit. Paul does not explicitly state the reason for the duality of the methods, but perhaps that is because prayer and praise are far more involved than merely transmitting knowledge. Understood as a holistic means of communicating with God, prayer and praise are also profound and intimate means of communication that go far beyond the transmitting of knowledge. Therefore, it seems fitting that a transcendent God would provide his creatures with a means of prayer and praise that transcends human boundaries of speech. Consequently, most Pentecostals have understood speaking in tongues as the "groanings too deep for words"

15. Lim, *Spiritual Gifts*, 147.

referred to in Rom 8:26.[16] Therefore, just as speaking in tongues results in the single believing individual offering prayer and praise to God, speaking in tongues within the corporate assembly of believers should result in the offering of prayer and praise to God.

It has become commonplace within some Pentecostal groups that the interpretation is a prophetic "message in tongues." There is, however, no evidence within Paul's instructions concerning the interpretation of tongues that indicate it should result in some special "prophetic message" to the assembly. If an interpretation of tongues is supposed to result in a "prophetic message" for the congregation, then the gift of interpretation becomes undifferentiable from the gift of prophecy. Furthermore, it forces a prophetic utterance to be contingent on speaking in tongues, which is not a biblical prerequisite for the gift of prophecy to function within the church. To this point, Fee states:

> Although it is quite common in Pentecostal groups to refer to a "message in tongues," there seems to be no evidence from Paul for such terminology. The tongues speaker is not addressing fellow believers, but God. This means that Paul understands the phenomenon basically to be prayer and praise.[17]

Unfortunately, the interpretation of tongues being used as a divine "prophetic message" takes the place of the proper function of the gift of prophecy within the church. Instead, the interpretation of tongues within the local assembly should result in the local congregation being united in understanding how they should corporately offer prayer and praise to God.

Not only this, but the use of the interpretation of speaking in tongues for a corporate "prophetic message" is wholly different from its function within the individual believer, which Paul clearly identifies as prayer and praise (1 Cor 14:14, 15). The interpretation of tongues that results in a "prophetic message" is a duplication of the gift of prophecy. It also changes the function of speaking in tongues to be wholly different than the proper function of speaking in tongues (prayer and praise to God). In addition, the practice of glossolalic interpretations which result in a "prophetic message" has no scriptural support.

Further evidence that the interpretation of corporate speaking in tongues should not result in a "prophetic message" can be found in the

16. Macchia, "Sighs Too Deep," 59.

17. Fee, *God's Empowering Presence*, 218.

fact that Paul stresses the supremacy of prophecy over speaking in tongues. In fact, while Paul encourages the practice of speaking in tongues, he clearly expresses the idea that prophecy is more profitable than speaking in tongues within the church (1 Cor 14:5–6). If speaking in tongues and its ensuing interpretation resulted in a prophetic utterance, Paul would not need to distinguish between the interpretation of tongues and prophecy. However, if the interpretation of speaking in tongues is prayer and praise to God, then the role of prophecy is clearly distinguishable from the function of speaking in tongues within the church. As such, whether performed privately or as a part of a corporate setting, glossolalia's fundamental purpose should remain the same: prayer and praise to God. The only meaningful distinction is that within the corporate assembly, interpretation is necessary in order for the congregation to understand how to direct their prayer and praise. In contrast, there is no need for interpretation when speaking in tongues is performed in private (1 Cor 14:16).

FRAMEWORK #4—THE PRIORITY OF LOVE

Even a cursory overview of 1 Cor 12–14 will reveal that chapter 13 is intentionally positioned in the middle of Paul's discourse regarding spiritual manifestations. In the midst of expounding on the proper function of spiritual gifts, Paul interjects love's central role. It is clear, then, that a discussion surrounding spiritual gifts without divine love at the center renders the "power" to be gained through possessing such virtues meaningless. In discussing 1 Cor 13 and love's central role within the spiritual gifts, Amos Yong writes:

> Not only are the manifestations nothing without love (13:2–3), but love neither ends nor fails (13:8), and it remains the greatest (13:13) expression of the church. Fundamentally the desire for the manifestation of the Spirit should be encouraged only if the members of the body follow and pursue after the way of redemptive love (14:1).[18]

Paul's deliberate placement of chapter 13's discourse on love provides an essential framework for helping us understand the function of all spiritual manifestations, including glossolalia. So, while not minimizing the role of charismata, Paul simultaneously reveals a "more excellent way" of love

18. Yong, *Renewing Christian Theology*, 71.

as the basis for all functions of spiritual manifestations. Simply put, chapter 13 provides a cutting rebuke to this Corinthian church which was more focused on spiritual manifestations than on loving one another. Fee states, "The Corinthian believers' passion for tongues in the assembly was further indication of their failure to love one another. Love, however, is not set forth in contrast to tongues, but as the necessary ingredient for the expression of all Spirit gifting."[19] Without divine love, all frameworks for spiritual manifestations will quickly fall into disarray and become of no spiritual value to any individual believer or the church as a whole.

Paul begins chapter 13 with the subject of speaking in tongues by referring to this phenomenon as "the tongues of angels" (1 Cor 13:1). Because the context suggests that the expression mentioned above refers to speaking in tongues, it is significant that "tongues of men" would also be equated as being of no value without love. In other words, if either speaking in tongues or normative human speech is done without love, it results in the same unproductive outcome. To further emphasize the superiority of love compared to all spiritual manifestations, Paul explains that if he possessed complete prophetic understanding without love, he would have nothing. Therefore, without love, the power of spiritual manifestations has no value to either the Lord or the local assembly. To this point, Keener explains:

> Spiritual power without love is dangerous, but love without some degree of spiritual power to carry forth its designs is impotent. Once our hearts are attuned to God's heart in love, we can seek various spiritual gifts for his glory, for serving our brothers and sisters in Christ, and for chaining the world around us that desperately needs transformation by Christ's power.[20]

The use of spiritual manifestations is not about the miraculous wonder of their operation but about allowing the Spirit to transform hearts and lives into a deeper loving relationship with God. Paul's argument to the Corinthians is that love must be the end goal of all spiritual manifestations. For if spiritual manifestations cease to be done in love, they no longer retain their spiritual nature and quickly devolve into carnal manifestations. This is precisely the problem that Paul is addressing in Corinth. Spiritual manifestations (specifically speaking in tongues) were not bringing edification to the church because of the Corinthians' lack of love. The result of such unloving manifestations was that the Corinthian church tolerated or endorsed

19. Fee, *First Epistle*, 634.

20. Keener, *Gift and Giver*, 135.

illicit sexuality, greed, and idolatry.[21] Therefore, it is through this discussion of love that Paul is striving to redirect the Corinthians' distorted view of spiritual manifestations and place it within the broader ethical context of Christlike character.[22] By doing this, Paul establishes that the value of spiritual manifestations proceeds only from within the context of believers who first love God and the church.

Additionally, cessationists often assume that Paul's statement "but when the perfect comes, the partial will be done away" refers to the canon of Scripture (1 Cor 13:9). However, this is a critical exegetical error, for Scripture cannot mean what it never meant to its original audience. The canon of Scripture is clearly not what the Corinthian church would have understood Paul to be addressing. Instead, the Corinthians would have understood Paul's reference to the arrival of the "perfect" as indicating our future eschatological hope. It is Paul's intent to help the Corinthians understand that the condition of the coming age will be one in which spiritual manifestations will no longer be necessary. However, the fact that they will no longer be required in that future, perfected state does nothing to negate their necessity in this present age. For as long as we live in an unperfected state, spiritual manifestations will be a vital requirement for the church to fulfill its mission.

While some cessationists point to 1 Cor 13:8 as "proof" that Paul taught that spiritual manifestations (specifically speaking in tongues) would cease, this case is made at the expense of ignoring the broader context of 1 Cor 12–14. When everything is taken into account, a Pauline theology of spiritual manifestations supports the practice of speaking in tongues within the diversity of spiritual manifestations within the church.

Paul's point regarding spiritual manifestations and their connection to love is that these manifestations will only cease at the end of the church age. There will be no need for spiritual manifestations in the new epoch because the church will have already performed its divine purpose. However, Paul reminds the Corinthians that when this time arrives, love will still be in operation as the bride of Christ enters the fullness of God's glorious kingdom. The overarching purpose of Paul inserting chapter 13 into the discussion of spiritual manifestations is not to condemn spiritual manifestations but instead to reorient them and put them into eschatological perspective.[23]

21. Horton, *I & II Corinthians*, 125.

22. Morton, "Gifts," 12.

23. Fee, *First Epistle*, 713.

Paul insists that spiritual manifestations, even the most remarkable, should not be viewed as an end in and of themselves. Instead, they must be viewed through a larger framework that centers on the ethic of love, Christ's love. This broader framework affirms the use of spiritual manifestations within this present epoch while also recognizing God's larger eschatological purposes.

CONCLUSION

Seen within the frameworks of unity within diversity, edification for order, prayer and praise, and the ethic of love, speaking in tongues can be viewed as a valuable and valued spiritual manifestation that operates within the church today. These frameworks that Paul lays out in his epistle to the church at Corinth are designed to serve as guardrails for all spiritual manifestations, but specifically for the phenomenon of speaking in tongues. These frameworks are not simply good suggestions but scriptural principles that the modern-day Christian should earnestly seek to abide in. While the Pentecostal is right to emphasize the importance of spiritual manifestations, they must also recognize that they cannot be more spiritual than they are scriptural. Through adhering to Paul's four frameworks, the Pentecostal can authoritatively stand on scriptural support for speaking in tongues within the church.

For Pentecostals, speaking in tongues has a profound influence on the way in which they live out their faith. Because of this, Pentecostals should recognize the value of the practice both within personal and corporate settings. The phenomenon of speaking in tongues is far more than a novel practice, having significant implications for how Pentecostals develop their practical theology. Because belief and behavior are intrinsically tied together, Pentecostals must be conscious of the truth that their biblical/theological approach to speaking in tongues will undoubtedly impact their practical theology.

3

A Practical Theology Perspective
of Speaking in Tongues

PENTECOSTAL PRACTICAL THEOLOGY

In defining the function of practical theology, Mark Cartledge writes, "It connects the use of scripture and its experience by means of the person and work of the Holy Spirit."[1] From the beginning of Pentecostalism, a strong emphasis was made on the experiential aspects of Christian life within the Spirit. A Pentecostal theology is not limited to a list of theological beliefs but insists on exploring Spirit-inspired orthodoxy within the context of Spirit-inspired orthopraxy. Therefore, the results of Spirit baptism include an awareness of the presence of God and an experience of the kingdom of God in power.

In other words, the heart of Pentecostal practical theology involves an experience *in* the Spirit that flows *from* Scripture. To this point, Menzies writes, "Pentecostal experience and practice is driven and shaped by the bible, particularly the narrative of Acts. It is impossible to understand Pentecostals apart from this basic, fundamental fact."[2] To be sure, Pentecostals see the work of the Spirit through the early church as the normative pattern for the church throughout this present age. This has caused Pentecostals historically to emphasize the necessity of practical theology by maintaining the importance of experiencing the Spirit as an active force in the believer's life.

1. Cartledge, *Charismatic Glossolalia*, 13.
2. Menzies, *Pentecost*, 9.

The biblical pattern of the working of the Holy Spirit in the life of the believer provides definite proof that there is an experiential reality to the receiving of the Holy Spirit. The presence of Spirit-induced empowerment involves experiential signs and wonders of the kingdom of God that should be practically evident in the everyday lives of Pentecostal believers.

Thus, practical theology demands that theology go beyond expounding truths and be placed within the contemporary practice of the Christian life. T. F. Torrance addresses the importance of practical theology:

> As the incarnate presence of the living God in space and time, Christ presents himself to our faith as its living, dynamic Object. This has the effect of calling for a living theology, a way of thinking which is at the same time a way of living, that cannot be abstracted from the life-giving acts of Christ in the depths of human being and must, therefore, affect man radically in his daily life and activity.[3]

Simply put, practical theology is a theology of action. One which examines the effects of God within the course of human history and critically reflects on the manner in which humanity should act in response to God's self-revelation. Therefore, a Pentecostal approach to practical theology must include an experiential connection by means of the person and work of the Holy Spirit.[4]

The Pentecostal experience of Spirit baptism is, first and foremost, an encounter with Jesus Christ. At its core, Pentecostalism is not Spirit centered but Christ centered, for the work of the Spirit centers on exalting Christ.[5] That encounter, mediated by the Spirit, changes the Spirit-baptized believer in physically observable ways. Even a cursory overview of the biblical account of glossolalic activity reveals that everyone who experienced Spirit baptism did so in ways that made it abundantly clear that something supernatural had occurred. Therefore, Pentecostals would deny any work of Spirit baptism that does not result in an evident, external sign of Christ's arrival.

It is precisely this evidential encounter with God that characterizes Pentecostals as people who are radically open to the Spirit. Because it is inherently a risky proposition to encounter God, the process of engaging a holy, transcendent God requires from unholy human beings a certain level

---

3. Torrance, *Reality and Evangelical Theology*, 138.

4. Cartledge, *Charismatic Glossolalia*, 3.

5. Menzies, *Pentecost*, 26.

of trepidation. In a real sense, speaking in tongues symbolizes this risk, for it requires that one surrender control of their most defining organ: the tongue (Jas 3:1–12; Prov 18:21).[6] Therefore, a Pentecostal practical theology of speaking in tongues recognizes the phenomenon as a divinely inspired mode of engaging with transcendency, resulting in a profound openness to the Spirit. The Pentecostal has found that whatever cost may be associated with surrendering to Spirit baptism as evidenced by speaking in tongues, the rewards of Spirit empowerment have been well worth it.

Pentecostal practical theology properly understood can be characterized as the pursuit of living the fullness of the gospel. The full gospel of the Pentecostal centers around the themes of salvation, sanctification, Spirit baptism, spiritual gifts, and kingdom fullness. The Pentecostal insistence that speaking in tongues be connected with Spirit baptism, spiritual gifts, and kingdom fullness should not be confused with the Spirit's work in regeneration. Instead, speaking in tongues from a Pentecostal perspective serves as a sign of Spirit empowerment that facilitates believers to live out the practical experience of their Spirit baptism.

This chapter will examine the way in which speaking in tongues practically influences four specific aspects: prayer, praise, missional empowerment, and eschatological hope. In the first section, the connection between speaking in tongues and prayer will be examined to understand how Spirit-filled prayer influences the day-to-day life of the Pentecostal. Next, an examination of the relationship between glossolalia and praise will be addressed to discover the manner in which Spirit-filled worship affects the practical experience of a Pentecostal. Additionally, speaking in tongues will be examined to show how the phenomenon relates to missional empowerment to understand how Spirit-filled living enhances a Pentecostal's ability to be missionally focused. Finally, this chapter will assess the practical theology of glossolalia by examining its connection to eschatological hope.

SPEAKING IN TONGUES AS A MODE OF PRAYER

The biblical definition of speaking in tongues is prayer and praise to God (1 Cor 14:13–19), and as such, the act of praying in the mode of glossolalic speech can be accurately referred to as praying in the Spirit (Eph 6:18; Jude 1:17–25). From a Pentecostal perspective, the connection between prayer and Spirit baptism can be identified as a vital lens through which

6. Menzies, *Speaking in Tongues*, 6.

Pentecostals view and order the other elements of the full gospel.[7] Thus, baptism in the Holy Spirit is inseparably tied to a transformational experience that takes place in and through prayer.

Speaking in tongues as a mode of Spirit-inspired prayer provides a practical reminder to the Pentecostal practitioner of their inherent weakness when approaching divinity. Viewed in this light, glossolalic prayer allows the practitioner to expresses a profound sense of humility before God by recognizing our utter frailty in communicating to God. In explaining the depth of this point, Menzies writes:

> Our inability to know how or what to pray is a stark reminder of our weaknesses. We realize that we cannot begin to express the longings and desires that the Spirit has birthed in our hearts. We sense that we are incapable of comprehending God's holiness and love. We do not know how to pray for our own needs or the needs of others. Yet, in the midst of our weakness, the Spirit intercedes for us and through us, utilizing words that have no meaning to us. Our speech reflects our yearning and thus emerges as "groans."[8]

While the human spirit desires intimate communication with God, we are bound by inherent physical inhibitors that limit our ability to communicate. While we cannot altogether remove these physical limitations, we are afforded the ability to communicate beyond these limitations through glossolalic prayer. When speaking in tongues as a mode of prayer, our spirit, guided by the Spirit, can communicate directly, enabling a temporary suspension of the physical limitations of language and knowledge. When we have no language that can adequately express our spirit's innermost desires, glossolalic prayer enables the practitioner to express these feelings to God. When we do not know what to pray about, glossolalic prayer offers us the ability to pray beyond our limited knowledge, to speak "mysteries in the Spirit" (1 Cor 14:2). Speaking in tongues as a form of Spirit-inspired prayer is powerful in a myriad of ways, but it is instrumental in dealing with spiritual warfare.

For both Paul and Jude, the context of praying in the Spirit is connected to its essential role in spiritual warfare (Eph 6:18; Jude 1:17–25). In concluding his discussion of the nature of the armor of God, Paul admonishes his readers to pray in the Spirit. The implication is clear that one weapon that should be functional within spiritual warfare is glossolalic prayer.

---

7. Vondey, *Pentecostal Theology*, 83.

8. Menzies, *Speaking in Tongues*, 163.

According to Paul, this form of prayer allows the pray-er to "utter mysteries" by the Spirit (1 Cor 14:2). Since glossolalic prayer is prayer directed toward God, the "words" spoken in the Spirit have equal power (some would argue more power) than those expressed with a known tongue.

From a biblical perspective, speaking in tongues as a prayer mode is Spirit-inspired prayer because it is a prayer initiated and guided by the Holy Spirit. For Paul, speaking in tongues is a vehicle for Spirit-inspired prayer. It is spiritual prayer, not mental; thus, praying in tongues is made up of utterances that transcend the limits of human conceptualization.[9] Glossolalic prayer is a beautiful union of human and divine prayer as Spirit-filled individuals allow the Spirit to pray through them. This powerful union of Spirit-directed prayer is both empowering in spiritual warfare and personally transformational. This explains the reason for Pentecostals' radical openness to God's presence and power. Having encountered God's presence in Spirit-inspired prayer, the Pentecostal understands the experiential transformation that takes place through this mode of communication.[10]

In discussing the practical nature of speaking in tongues, the apostle Paul explicitly describes the action of praying in tongues as "praying with my spirit" (1 Cor 14:14–16). In describing glossolalic prayer as flowing from "my spirit," Paul reveals that Spirit praying functions in accord with the spirit of man (Acts 2:2). Some wrongly assume that glossolalic prayer happens due to the Spirit "taking over" a person's will and forcing them to speak in tongues. However, this is not the biblical pattern expressed through the Scriptures. Instead, the Spirit works in union with the human will in order to mold their will to his. Thus, the Pentecostal approach to prayer views this sacramental action as more than just an external force; it is a force designed to empower the inner spirit (Eph 3:16).

This means that glossolalic prayer should be understood as one of the Spirit's instruments for empowering the Christian's spiritual life. Since all disciples of Christ are engaged in spiritual warfare, praying in the Spirit serves as a spiritual weapon that assists us in our weaknesses (Rom 8:26–27), enables us to know the mind of the Spirit (1 Cor 2:10–16), and opens our will to God's (Eph 1:17–18).

Fee discusses Paul's teachings on this matter by stating:

> It is probably impossible to understand Paul as a theologian
> if one does not take this dimension of this spirituality with full

9. Williams, *Renewal Theology*, 218.

10. Cross, "Divine-Human Encounter," 7.

seriousness. A prayerless life is one of practical atheism. As one who lived in and by the Spirit, Paul understood prayer, in particular, to be the special prompting of the Spirit, leading him to thanksgiving for others and petition in the Spirit, even when he did not know for what specifically to pray. Whatever else life in the Spirit meant for Paul, it meant a life devoted to prayer.[11]

Pentecostals view prayer as more than merely a monologue to God—it is an opportunity to experience a divine dialogue through the Spirit. As part of this divine dialogue, the Spirit plays an essential role in aiding Christians in their practical living in the Spirit. It should also be pointed out that prayer in the Spirit is not biblically required to be done in ecstasy. While there is undoubtedly room for praying in the Spirit with great exuberance, the goal of praying in the Spirit is not to elicit an emotional reaction (although this is undoubtedly a by-product). Instead, the goal is to facilitate Spirit-filled living in the pray-er. Therefore, when examining glossolalic prayers, the question should not be "What does this mode of prayer sound like?" but instead "What does this mode of prayer do?" Glossolalic prayer is far less about saying something and much more about doing something.[12] Glossolalic prayer should be seen as a function of the Spirit doing an infusion of the power of God in a visible manner into the life of the believer. As such, glossolalic prayer offers a powerful method for a person to become both receptive to and a conduit of the Spirit's work.

To this point, it is essential to note that speaking in tongues (like other forms of prayer) is fundamentally amoral apart from its connection to the Spirit. This means that there is nothing inherently spiritual about glossolalic prayer, but its "spiritual" nature flows only from its relationship to the Spirit. In other words, there are no inherent mystical "powers" associated with speaking in tongues. Instead, its power lies solely in the fact that through this action, our spirit is being connected to the Spirit. This can be understood by comparing glossolalic prayer with prayer done in a known tongue. Prayers being offered up in a known tongue do not have "power" based on the pray-ers words. Instead, the power resides in the One to whom we are praying. From this perspective, it is clear that the words themselves are but a minimal component of the act of prayer. Within the act of prayer, the pray-er does not receive spiritual power based upon the words used but solely based upon the fact that their spirit is connecting

11. Fee, *People of God*, 53.

12. Smith, *Thinking in Tongues*, 142.

with the Spirit of God. Likewise, the act of glossolalic prayer does not infuse power into the practitioner's life based upon the "words" of speaking in tongues. Instead, the power of glossolalic prayer resides solely in the fact that the practitioner's spirit is being united with the Spirit of God in life-giving communication.

Furthermore, while some theologians would want to classify all prayer as a spiritual act, all prayer should not be classified as spiritual prayer from a biblical perspective. Prayers offered to false gods are, in fact, not spiritual at all. While these prayers may appear to be spiritual because the actions being done look spiritual, if they lack spiritual life, it is impossible for these "prayers" to possess any spiritual life (Eph 2:2; 1 Cor 8:8). Similarly, just as one can perform the act of prayer devoid of spiritual life, so it is possible for one to speak in tongues devoid of the spiritual life of God. Just as there is a counterfeit prayer that lacks the Spirit's power, it is possible that glossolalic "prayer" could take place devoid of the life of the Spirit.

Because of this truth, some would seek to discredit speaking in tongues as a valid sign of Spirit baptism. The argument goes like this: If speaking in tongues can be practiced outside of the Spirit, then how can it possibly serve as the initial sign of Spirit-baptism reception? However, this attempt to discredit the clear biblical evidence of speaking in tongues accompanying Spirit baptism on the basis that it can be counterfeited is to commit a logical error. First, it fails to recognize the fact that there are examples of counterfeit associations with every other biblically supported work of God. For instance, counterfeit gospels promote and spread an anti-biblical gospel; counterfeit salvations promote a works-based means of grace; counterfeit forms of worship promote the worship of man or idols. However, it would be illogical to assert that simply because there is a counterfeit to a biblically based belief, we should then reject the biblically based position. Instead, a logical response is that the Christian affirms the biblically supported position while at the same time confronting the existence of the counterfeit. In fact, it is only through the lens of a biblically based approach that we can recognize the counterfeit and defend against its presence.

From a Pentecostal perspective, prayer evokes our affections and goes beyond the mere words spoken in prayer to include that which is experienced by prayer. It follows, then, that glossolalic prayer is indispensable to the practical theological process since through it the pray-er's affections are connected to the Spirit (Rom 8:26). In fact, according to Land, prayer is the Pentecostal's primary theological activity. Prayer keeps theology from departing from the Spirit and develops deeper hunger for the Spirit that motivates the believer toward a gospel-centered life.[13] Unsurprisingly, it is precisely this Spirit-induced act of speaking in tongues that sets aflame the believer's affections in prayer and releases the innermost expressions of worship to God. Undoubtedly, this spiritual prayer life has been the driving force that has allowed Pentecostalism to grow at such historically unprecedented rates.

A Pentecostal practical theology of speaking in tongues not only recognizes the immense power of prayer but also appreciates the role that Spirit-inspired worship plays in the formation of Pentecostalism. The fact that Pentecostals are known for exuberant worship is not a random association. Instead, the Pentecostal is aware that the phenomenon of speaking in tongues is intrinsically tied with the action of worship.

SPEAKING IN TONGUES AS A MODE OF PRAISE

The apostle Paul is clear that the activity of speaking in tongues encompasses more than Spirit-inspired prayer—it includes the act of Spirit-inspired praise. For Paul, glossolalic praise is not merely a theoretical supposition but is drawn from an active knowledge based on personal experience. The use of first-person pronouns in describing glossolalic praise reveals Paul's intimate knowledge that the phenomenon should be understood as the product of Spirit-directed activity within a person's life (1 Cor 14:14, 15, 18).

From the very first instance of Spirit baptism on the day of Pentecost (Acts 2), there is clear evidence that speaking in tongues is a way of offering praises to God. On the occasion of their reception of the Spirit, the disciples' tongue speech was so astounding that it gathered a crowd. Luke quotes these devout Jews as proclaiming:

> "Why, are not all these who are speaking Galileans? And how is it that we each hear them in our own language to which we were born? Parthians and Medes and Elamites, and residents of Mesopotamia, Judea and Cappadocia, Pontus and Asia, Phrygia and Pamphylia, Egypt and the districts of Libya around Cyrene, and visitors from Rome, both Jews and proselytes, Cretans and Arabs—we hear them in our own tongues speaking of *the mighty deeds of God.*" And they all continued in amazement and great

13. Land, *Pentecostal Spirituality*, 35.

perplexity, saying to one another, "What does this mean?" (Acts 2:7–12, italics mine)

It is evident that the glossolalic doxological speech of the disciples raised questions in the minds of these Jews. While they questioned how these uneducated Galileans could be speaking all of these foreign languages, they did not question the obvious fact that what they heard was praise to God. That was clear. Therefore, the central question for these Jewish diaspora members was how this supernatural praise to God originated from people they knew did not know these foreign dialects.

Similarly, in the account of the Roman centurion Cornelius and his household receiving Spirit baptism, the apostles heard them "speaking with tongues and exalting God" (Acts 10:46). The explicit linkage of glossolalia with worship in this account provides a powerful example of how glossolalic activity functions as a means of praising God. In summarizing the biblical use of glossolalic praise, Cartledge explains that tongue speech should be understood as a language that declares the wonders of God.[14] Later, Peter affirms that what those Gentile believers received corresponded to what the 120 received on the day of Pentecost (Acts 11:15). Additionally, Paul supports the use of speaking in tongues as a means of worshiping God by affirming his personal use of "singing with the spirit" (1 Cor 14:15). And in admonishing the Ephesian church to be filled with the Spirit, he encourages them to do so in psalms, hymns, and spiritual songs (Eph 5:19). Addressing a Pauline perspective on the Spirit's role in worship, Fee observes, "For Paul, the gathered church was, first of all, a worshipping community; and the key to their worship was the presence of the Holy Spirit."[15] While Spirit-inspired worship should be evident within the church in multiple ways, one biblical mode of Spirit-induced worship is glossolalic speech.

In Paul's Letter to the Ephesians, a reference to singing in tongues can be seen, where Paul writes:

> And do not get drunk with wine, for that is dissipation, but be filled with the Spirit, speaking to one another in psalms and hymns and spiritual songs, singing and making melody with your heart to the Lord. (Eph 5:18–19)

These spiritual songs, or "spirit-induced" songs, serve as a likely example of glossolalic praise. Two essential factors suggest that Paul had in mind

14. Cartledge, *Mediation of the Spirit*, 96.
15. Fee, *People of God*, 153.

glossolalic singing. First, the fact that this type of praise is contrasted with the charge to "not get drunk with wine" suggests the temptation to arrive at ecstatic praise through the stimulus of drink. While Paul indeed allows exuberant or spontaneous worship, these impulses must originate from the Spirit and not through carnal means. This is likely a reference to the accusation made on the day of Pentecost, where the amazed crowd assumed the Spirit-baptized disciples were drunk (Acts 2:13). Secondly, Paul's distinguishing of spiritual songs from psalms and hymns suggests that these spiritual songs are somehow quite different in nature from the other two forms of praise. The word "spiritual" describes the song and the fact that the one singing has been prompted by the Spirit, thus manifesting an act of the Spirit as they sing in tongues.[16]

It should be no surprise, then, that Pentecostals emphasize the importance of Spirit-led worship in their private and corporate worship times. In explaining the diversity of worship within the Pentecostal community, Kärkkäinen writes, "Pentecostal worshipping communities display their love of God through a wide variety of spiritual practices, such as tongues-speaking, prophetic utterances, healing prayers, and supernatural encounters with God."[17] The prominent theme of worship in Pentecostal theology is focused on the idea that the Spirit is the one who is active in the world, bringing a tangible experience of life to believers. Therefore, the Holy Spirit makes Pentecostal spirituality a reality in worship and the driving force that connects orthodoxy and orthopraxy.[18] Unquestionably, this emphasis on the role of the Spirit provides Pentecostals with an openness to the moving of the Spirit.

This foundational belief regarding the Spirit's involvement in the worship of believers inspires Pentecostals to agree with the apostle Paul's assessment of the value of speaking in tongues as a form of praise to God (1 Cor 14:5, 15, 18). While most Pentecostals are familiar with praying in tongues, many have failed to appreciate the equally important benefits of praising in tongues. Paul permits Spirit-inspired worship both in a known tongue and through the use of glossolalic utterances (1 Cor 14:15); for this reason, Pentecostals should affirm the practice of both modes. By validating both modes of worship as credible forms of expressing praise to God, Paul provides a clear orthopraxy for glossolalic worship. Acknowledging

16. Dunn, *Jesus and the Spirit*, 238.

17. Kärkkäinen, *Introduction to Ecclesiology*, 13.

18. Land, *Pentecostal Spirituality*, 23.

the practical implication of glossolalic worship significantly broadens the biblical definition of worship—both within the context of personal worship and within the communal practice of offering praise to God.

Indeed, speaking in tongues provides Pentecostalism with not only a distinct way of worshiping but also a distinct way of thinking about worship. Embedded in Pentecostal practice is not only a spirituality but also something like a worldview.[19] Therefore, whether within the context of a worship service or as part of the private devotional life, the practice of speaking in tongues as a mode of worship to God has an essential place within the practical theology of Pentecostalism. As creatures designed by God to worship, Pentecostals fully embrace the Spirit's aid in accomplishing this divine mandate (John 4:23–24). Therefore, it is through the participation of Spirit-led worship that the church is unified in corporate worship to God.

In the act of glossolalic worship, the practitioner can express their worship in Spirit-directed ways that move their worship beyond the contrasts of language to utter the mysteries of the Spirit (1 Cor 14:2). As Spirit-directed worship, speaking in tongues as a form of worship offers a deep intimacy within worship. Free from the limitation of language, glossolalic worship allows the spirit of humanity to connect directly to the Spirit in worship. With this understanding, Pentecostals need not be ashamed of their distinctive practice of glossolalic worship. Instead, this practice should boldly testify to the glorious wonder and supernatural empowerment provided through glossolalic worship. As Pentecostals reflect on the Spirit-inspired possibilities afforded by glossolalic worship, they continue to discover an ever-increasing expression of intimate praises to an infinite God.

Furthermore, a receptiveness to the Spirit's influence to empower the act of worship allows for increased openness to the Spirit's formation in other areas of the believer's life. Since missional theology naturally flows from one's theology of worship, it is precisely this attention to Spirit-induced worship that provides a catalyst toward Spirit dependency for missional empowerment. Without question, from a Pentecostal theology of worship, it is Spirit-empowered worship that motivates believers for mission. In other words, bold witness flows out of Spirit-empowered praise. It is not surprising, then, that Pentecostalism's emphasis on Spirit baptism has resulted in its being one of the leading missionary movements in the world.

19. Smith, *Thinking in Tongues*, 24.

This is not an arbitrary connection but a direct consequence of Pentecostalism's prominent placing of glossolalia within its worship.

Because Pentecostals interpret worship in connection with the Acts of the Apostles, the heart of Pentecostal worship is motivated and driven by the Spirit. In addressing the ways in which a Pentecostal theology of charisma—and glossolalic speech specifically—influences Pentecostalism's missional focus, Robert Menzies writes, "Every time we speak in tongues or hear glossolalia in our worship services, it should remind us that God desires that every person on the planet should have the opportunity to hear the gospel."[20] In other words, from a Pentecostal perspective, to worship through speaking in other tongues should not take place without also profoundly reflecting on the unreached people groups of the world.

SPEAKING IN TONGUES AS MISSIONAL EMPOWERMENT

At the heart of practical theology is its missional focus. It is the missiological dimension that provides the aims, the goals, the methods, the necessary motives, and the vision to guide the task of practical theology.[21] The fact that the outpouring of the Spirit on the day of Pentecost had a transformational impact on the disciples was immediately apparent. Beginning with the boldness of Peter's expositional sermon at Pentecost, the entirety of the Acts of the Apostles reveals the impact of the Spirit's indwelling power enabling the disciples to fulfill Christ's command to spread the gospel (Matt 28:19–20). Yet, the explosion of this missional movement came in the face of numerous hardships and constant persecution (Acts 8:1). Knowing that the road ahead for the early church would be anything but easy, Christ commanded the disciples to be baptized in the Spirit so that they might receive the supernatural power (δύναμις) and comfort (παράκλητος) required to fulfill his kingdom purposes on this earth.

Pentecostals have historically seen the baptism of the Holy Spirit as evidenced by speaking in tongues as the critical factor for providing missional empowerment. As a restorative movement, the Pentecostal movement since its inception has been a sending agency characterized by "signs and wonders," most notably that of speaking in tongues. To this point, Menzies writes:

20. Menzies, *Speaking in Tongues*, 160.

21. Anderson, *Ministry on the Fireline*, 31.

> We Pentecostals have always read the narrative of Acts, and particularly the account of the Pentecostal outpouring of the Holy Spirit (Acts 2), as a model for our own lives. We find encouragement in the way that God uses unschooled and ordinary people to advance His cause. We revel in stories of simple fishermen who are called and enabled to bear bold witness for Jesus. We delight in the account of poor peasants persevering in the midst of great opposition and suffering, These stories become our stories and encourage us also to live lives marked by extraordinary faith, the willingness to hazard risks, and a deep desire to exalt the name of Jesus.[22]

In both his gospel account and his historical account, a Pentecostal missiological perspective of Luke's writing views the Holy Spirit as the source of inspiration in speech that empowers God's people for effective service.[23] Therefore, Luke's primary focus in his two-volume account is to depict the Spirit first and foremost as the driving force of redemptive history. This perspective underscores the fact that Christ did not leave the early church to its own devices. Instead, by means of Spirit baptism, Christ empowered his disciples to represent him among the nations (Acts 1:8). In this way, Spirit baptism on the day of Pentecost became a "first fruit" of this promise as the Spirit broke forth in visible power.

A Pentecostal ecclesiology centers on the idea that God has commissioned the church as a sent and sending community. Given the fact that Pentecostals use Acts as a paradigm through which to view their missional purpose, it seems logical that they would expect to experience similar empowerment from the Spirit. Through the Spirit, this society of evangelists is to experience supernatural empowerment as the actualizing force behind its mission throughout this world. In this way, speaking in tongues does more than serve as a sign of Spirit baptism; it also offers a physical symbol of the Spirit empowering work for witness. Therefore, the practice of speaking in tongues energizes the practitioner for mission by divinely empowering them to effectively "declare the wonders of God" (Acts 2:11).

What is clear from a careful reading of Luke is that the Spirit's indwelling should not be understood as merely an internal force in the life of the believer; the Spirit's work also includes external manifestations. Arthur Glasser explains:

22. Menzies, *Speaking in Tongues*, 2.
23. Menzies, *Empowered for Witness*, 44.

> In Acts, whenever mention is made of believers being filled with the Holy Spirit, the account always goes on to mention speech (Acts 2:2; 4:8, 31; 7:55–56; 9:17–20: 10:44–46; 13:9–10; 13:52–14:1; 19:6). Whereas it is true that the fruit of the Spirit described in Galatians 5:22–23 is largely his provision of inward grace, Acts would have us understand that a primary work of the Spirit is to open people's mouths and get them to bear witness to Jesus Christ.[24]

Therefore, for Pentecostals, Acts is not merely a historical document to be examined for its historicity alone but a model for the life of the contemporary church. A Pentecostal missiological perspective views the presence of the Spirit as the driving force which propels into mission, enlivens worship, and increases consecration for the coming of the Lord of the harvest.[25] In this way, Pentecostals view speaking in tongues as a sign that the early Christians' experience in Acts is also our experience and that the narrative of Acts should provide a road map for living a spirit-empowered witness.[26]

The fact that Luke stresses the connection between the working of the Spirit and an external act of speech that empowers believers for missional work is no accident. Speaking in tongues is logically connected to Luke's emphasis on baptism in the Spirit as empowerment for mission; therefore, it is not an arbitrary sign but rather an essential sign.[27] Luke's account, therefore, strongly suggests that all Spirit-filled believers must possess the capacity to speak and act in accordance with Christ's mission. Luke further highlights the missional nature of speaking in tongues through Peter's prophetic explanation of the events at Pentecost. Since speaking in tongues accompanies the Spirit empowerment of those at Pentecost, it is evident that this association was a missional sign for Luke.[28] Thus, Pentecost served as the foundation for the mission theology of the early church, and this mission theology directly influences the overall theology of the church.

To this point, several critical theological implications need to be addressed within a Pentecostal theology of speaking in tongues and how it connects to missional empowerment. First, the fact that Luke ties charisma to the missional empowerment of the early church demands that present-day Christians take seriously the Pentecostal insistence that charisma is for

---

24. Glasser, *Announcing the Kingdom*, 263.

25. Land, *Pentecostal Spirituality*, 65.

26. Menzies, *Speaking in Tongues*, 3.

27. Keener, "Spirit's Empowerment," 183.

28. Miller, *Missionary Tongues Revisited*, 60.

the church today. For the cessationist to presume that the Spirit empower-ment administered throughout the early church ceased with the apostles suggests that present-day disciples of Christ do not need the Spirit empow-erment essential to the first church's missional success. On the contrary, in the face of ever-increasing wickedness, the present-day church would be wise to recognize her utter dependence on Spirit empowerment. The clear biblical objective for the Spirit's outpouring at Pentecost was that the church might receive divine empowerment in order to complete its mis-sion in the world. It is precisely this reason that missional empowerment should be an indispensable necessity at all times.[29] Contrary to cessationist teachings, Spirit baptism (and all charismatic gifts) will only cease at the completion of this present epoch (1 Cor 13:8–10).

A Pentecostal theology of mission emphasizes that the missiological call to witness is that Spirit baptism leads one to embrace both the opportu-nity of and responsibility for mission and that this divine calling originates in and through the Spirit.[30] Keener observes,

> In whatever way he leads us, whether simply by emboldening us or giving us wisdom how best to share with a particular person, God's Spirit leads our witness. This is a major emphasis of the Pen-tecost story: We witness for Christ, and we depend on God's power to make our witness effective.[31]

The same Spirit continues to empower us, just as early Christians first ex-perienced the presence and power of Christ in their lives at Pentecost and then produced theological reflections based on that experience.[32]

This same Pentecost experience continues to shape the modern Pente-costal Church in its theological perspective of the missional directive of the church. To this point, Amos Yong suggests:

> The central role of the Acts narrative has continued to shape the missionary and evangelistic approaches of Pentecostal churches. If the outpouring of the Spirit on the Day of Pentecost resulted in the evangelization of the Mediterranean world, then the modern-day outpouring of the Holy Spirit is intended for the evangelization of the whole world.[33]

29. Keener, *Spirit Hermeneutics*, 49.

30. Yong, *Mission after Pentecost*, 188.

31. Keener, *Gift and Giver*, 57.

32. Anderson, *Ministry on the Fireline*, 101.

33. Yong, *Spirit Poured Out*, 78.

The centrality of the Spirit in mission has been a consistent theme in Pentecostal studies precisely because Pentecostals believe in seeking missional empowerment from the Spirit. The modern Pentecostal movement (like the early church) was from its commencement a missionary movement made possible by the Spirit's empowerment. The Pentecostal mission is grounded first and foremost in the conviction that the Holy Spirit is the motivating power behind all missional activity. Christ commanded the disciples to wait in Jerusalem for "power from on high" (Luke 24:49) and later promised them, "You will receive power when the Holy Spirit has come upon you; and you will be my witnesses in Jerusalem, in all Judea and Samaria, and to the ends of the earth" (Acts 1:8). Thus, the early church recognized their need for Spirit empowerment as an essential part of a missiological theology.

For the Pentecostal, the insistence on Spirit baptism is evidence of that same awareness: empowerment for mission. It is precisely this Spirit empowerment for witness that occurs at Spirit baptism, which empowers the people of God as prophets (people who speak for God). As a language of Spirit-inspired prayer and praise, speaking in tongues plays a unique role in the process of participating in the presence of God to empower the people of God for service. Therefore, the argument can be made that for Pentecostals to exchange tongues for some other "sign" of Spirit baptism cannot be done without losing something of its distinct missional theology in the process.

Pentecostal missiologist Paul Pomerville explains that the Lukan account in Acts reveals that obedience to the Great Commission (the emphasis of most Evangelicals) is not the primary motivation for missional theology for Pentecostals. The Holy Spirit poured out at Pentecost is a missionary Spirit, the church full of the Spirit is a missionary community, and the church's witness is "the release of an inward dynamic."[34] In other words, the emphasis of Pentecostal missiological theology is first a *missio Spiritus* that then naturally motivates one to be obedient to the Great Commission. Lesslie Newbigin argues this point by stating:

> Mission is not essentially an action by which the church puts forth its own power and wisdom to conquer the world around it; it is, rather, the action of God, putting forth the power of his Spirit to

---

34. Pomerville, *Third Force in Missions*, 65.

bring the universal work of Christ for the salvation of the world nearer to its completion.[35]

This *missio Spiritus* philosophical approach has enabled modern Pentecostalism to become a leading force in contemporary missiological theology. To give up the expectation of tongues as the initial physical evidence of Spirit baptism will undoubtedly result in the Pentecostal Church suffering the loss of its dimension of missional power. The missiological philosophy gleaned from Luke-Acts is unique to Pentecostals. While other Protestant groups have emphasized the Pauline epistles, Pentecostals have highlighted Luke-Acts.[36] Driving this philosophical approach is the Pentecostals' belief that they are a part of the continuation of the historicity of the Acts of the Apostles.

As a tangible symbol of Spirit-induced missional empowerment, speaking in tongues is viewed by Pentecostals as something that gives direction to their action and ties their current mission to the disciples' mission on the day of Pentecost. For the Pentecostal, the same bold witness of the deity of Jesus Christ that characterized the disciples at Pentecost is their primary calling and the central purpose of their Spirit-inspired experience.[37] Through speaking in tongues, the missional connection between the early church and the Pentecostal Church is not merely theoretical; in some real sense, speaking in tongues marks both groups as members of the prophet Joel's eschatological missional community. Stemming from a radical openness to Spirit-inspired missional speaking, Pentecostals continue to see the Acts of the Apostles (and specifically the day of Pentecost) as more than a mere historical account—as something that shapes and inspires our current missional activities.

For Pentecostals, the lack of formal closure to the book of Acts is an invitation to every reader in every place and in every epoch to participate in the work and witness of the Spirit of God. Thus, Pentecostals view themselves as a continuance of the missional work first reported in the Acts of the Apostles. The same Spirit who empowered the disciples is continuing to accomplish God's redemptive work in this world today. This ongoing missiological philosophy leads Pentecostals to participate in the *missio Spiritus* and remain open to being radically guided by the Spirit. Just as the outpouring on the day of Pentecost resulted in all those gathered in the upper room

35. Newbigin, *Open Secret*, 60.

36. Menzies, *Pentecost*, 118.

37. Menzies, *Speaking in Tongues*, 158.

being primary witnesses of the resurrected Jesus, through Spirit baptism Pentecostals see themselves as primary and not secondary witnesses of the missional work of Christ to save in this present world. Therefore, in every private and communal experience of speaking in tongues, the practitioner offers a tangible sign which reminds both the individual believer and the larger church body of our calling that we have received from Christ and the divine enabling that we have been promised by him (Acts 1:8).[38]

It is precisely this fundamental openness to the Spirit's power that enables Pentecostals to embrace a Lukan theology of the glossolalic phenomenon as a sign of Spirit baptism that immerses believers in the Spirit's work through missional empowerment. Therefore, speaking in tongues serves as the epistemological sign to the believer that he or she has been empowered to serve as a witness of the truth of the gospel (Acts 2:22–36). Moreover, speaking in tongues serves as a present "sign" to the church of the reality of the Spirit's eschatological presence (Acts 2:16–21). In this way, the Spirit facilitates the church's mission by bringing people, nations, and the whole world into eschatological perfection.

From a Pentecostal theological perspective, the day of Pentecost provides a powerful connection between the missional empowerment of the Holy Spirit and eschatological hope.[39] In this way, the Pentecostal *missio Spiritus* reaches beyond temporal missiological frameworks to influence both eschatological and apocalyptic philosophies. Eschatologically, speaking in tongues demonstrates the Spirit's working both in the here and now and what is to come. Apocalyptically, it discloses the truth of Jesus Christ in both the present and the ages to come.[40] The Spirit-empowered church serves as a "sign" of what is to come when God's kingdom is fully realized in the world.

SPEAKING IN TONGUES AS ESCHATOLOGICAL HOPE

Simply defined, eschatology is the examination of the fulfillment of God's promises to bring about the restoration of all things and to establish his kingdom forever (Isa 65:17; Rev 21:5). Therefore, eschatological hope is about more than merely "the end of the world." It centers on the idea of

---

38. Menzies, *Speaking in Tongues*, 4.

39. Cartledge, *Mediation of the Spirit*, 12.

40. Yong, *Mission after Pentecost*, 261.

heaven and earth being fully reunited under Christ's reign.[41] Ultimately, eschatology is not about the end of all things but about a new beginning, one in which the kingdom of God will appear in all its fullness (Rev 11:15).

From a historical perspective, eschatological hope has always maintained a prominent position in Pentecostal theology. Even at the movement's formation, Pentecostals emphasized eschatological themes in their worship, preaching, and missional emphasis.[42] As a result, Pentecostals cannot be rightly understood without appreciating how eschatological ideas have influenced their thoughts, actions, and passions.[43] Pentecostal theology is more than a set of beliefs to which one must ascribe mentally. Instead, Pentecostalism is inherently a practical theology because of the experiential nature that is fundamentally associated with Pentecostalism's view of the Spirit-filled life.

Given the above, it is no coincidence that Pentecostal theology has traditionally emphasized eschatological hope as the driving force in its worship and the motivation for missional engagement. Eschatology is not an afterthought in Pentecostalism but a vital constitutive part that drives the whole of Pentecostal theology. Within this framework, speaking in tongues should also be understood as more than a novel mode for expressing prayer and praise to God. Instead, speaking in tongues serves as an eschatological symbol of an epoch in which the kingdom of God will be fully realized. In explaining the importance of speaking in tongues as an apocalyptic sign of divine presence, Steven Land suggests:

> The distinctive apocalyptic affections of Pentecostalism will be shown to be the integrating core for its narrative beliefs and practices. But the decisive context and ever-present horizon for most usefully and comprehensibly displaying those beliefs, practices, and affections are eschatological: the presence of God who, as Spirit, is the agent of the in breaking, soon to be consummated kingdom of God.[44]

Within Pentecostal theology, the glossolalic phenomenon can also be seen as a Spirit-inspired theophany. As unconscious human speech, speaking in tongues becomes an instrument through which the Holy Spirit's

---

41. Althouse, *Spirit*, 110.

42. For more information about the history of Pentecostalism's eschatological focus, see Jacobson, *Reader in Pentecostal Theology*.

43. Johnson, "Fulfillment of God's Promise," 97.

44. Land, *Pentecostal Spirituality*, 12.

power can be demonstrated in this present age. Since glossolalic speech consists of both human and divine elements, it functions to unite the languages of heaven and earth. Speaking in tongues, then, becomes a powerful actualization of the union between humanity and the Spirit working in unity to glorify God through Spirit-directed prayer and praise.[45] The practical theological implications of speaking in tongues reveal that its practice has eschatological hope at its core. In addressing the practical theological connection between eschatology and the work of the Spirt, Macchia writes:

> If the Spirit is anything in the Bible, it is an eschatological gift. Recognizing that eschatology is richly pneumatological opens the door to seeing the flames that ignite eschatological passion as the flame of divine live through the rich and diverse presence of Christ among us and the future culmination of that redemptive love at Christ's coming. Participation in God is participation in the eschatological freedom of the divine life in history to move all things toward new creation.[46]

From this perspective, it is possible to view speaking in tongues as an apparent reversal of the division of languages at Babel (Gen 11:1–9) and as offering a glimpse into the future eschatological hope of the unification of all languages in worship toward God (Rev 7:9–10). The fact that on the day of Pentecost a miracle of linguistic reunification took place reveals the nature of God's eternal mercy. The confusion of speech came as the result of God's judgment upon humanity. Yet, through the tongue speech of the disciples at Pentecost, Luke provides an eschatological glimpse into our future hope. From a Pentecostal perspective, this eschatological hope is reaffirmed and rekindled in every generation through the continual practice of speaking in other tongues.

This all points to an eschatological period in which the mortal constraints on prayer and praise will no longer be felt. Through resurrected bodies, God's people will be able to commune with him free from the limitations of this present age (1 Cor 15). Therefore, in a practical sense, the presence of the eschatological Spirit (as experienced through speaking in tongues) serves as a foretaste of the coming fullness of the kingdom of God. This foretaste of uninhibited prayer and praise to God fills our hearts with "groanings too deep for words" (Rom 8:26) as we anticipate the realization of our eschatological hope. To this point, Macchia writes:

45. Stephenson, *Types of Pentecostal Theology*, 76.
46. Macchia, *Baptized in the Spirit*, 48.

Rather than tongues being a sign of an escape from this world into heights of glory, they are expressions of strength in weakness, or the capacity to experience the first-fruits of the kingdom-to-come in the midst of our groaning with the suffering creation.[47]

Seen within a Pentecostal theological framework, the act of speaking in tongues can be understood as a unique bridge that connects the church's historical past, its present, and its future eschatological hope. Through participating in both the tongues of men and of angels (1 Cor 13), glossolalic speech offers the practitioner an experiential glimpse into an eschatological time when prayer and praise will be perfected (1 Cor 13:10). Paul clarifies that within this coming perfected, eschatological age, the need for spiritual manifestation will no longer be required (1 Cor 13:8–10). The reality of speaking in tongues in this present age points to the eschatological hope of the coming age when it will no longer be necessary. Yet, until the arrival of our eschatological hope, speaking in tongues serves as a powerful conduit, providing believers with missional empowerment and the means to praise and pray to God in the Spirit.

As such, the praxis of the Spirit is not complete unless viewed in terms of God's eschatological fulfillment of the cosmos, not merely in terms of replicating the first-century church. In other words, a Pentecostal practical theology of speaking in tongues views the phenomenon as significant for both historical precedence *and* future precedence as it points toward the eschatological hope for the coming age. To this point, Macchia writes:

> Eschatology is helpful for showing the expansive reach of pneumatology, because eschatology implies a participation in God that is both purifying and empowering, presently at work and still unfulfilled, and life-transforming and demanding in terms of how we will respond to the reign of God in our times.[48]

At the beginning of time, the Spirit "communicates" through his divine breathing to create (Gen 1:2); at Pentecost, the same Spirit is communicating to the nations through glossolalic unction (Acts 2). Finally, at the end of John's revelation, the Spirit communicates a call for all the nations to be unified in the worship of God (Rev 22:17). Viewing Pentecost as an end-time event leads to eschatological hope that we can see Jesus as the Spirit baptizer bringing all humanity into eschatological reality. So, what we find

47. Macchia, "Groans Too Deep," 159.
48. Macchia, *Baptized in the Spirit*, 41.

in the eschatological framework of Revelation is that the culmination of the cosmos exposes that the ultimate *missio Dei* is communicated through the *missio Spiritus*. From the outpouring of the Spirit in Jerusalem at Pentecost to the eschatological hope of the new Jerusalem, the Spirit manifests its cosmic mission of gathering not just a diverse group of many language groups, but *all* language groups (Rev 5:9; 7:9; 14:6). Therefore, every expression of speaking in tongues can be seen as a beautiful foretaste of the ultimate reunification of human worship free from the present barrier of language divisions.

A Pentecostal understanding of the outpouring of the Spirit in Acts 2 must include its connection to the fulfillment of the prophet Joel's prophecy concerning eschatological events (Joel 2). Therefore, it should be recognized that the apostle Peter's message concerning the Spirit's arrival being "poured out on all flesh" (Joel 2:28; Acts 2:17) was physically realized through the glossolalic words of the disciples at Pentecost. Thus, in some real sense, the glossolalic utterances of the disciples that were heard by those of "every nation under heaven" (Acts 2:5) were but the first of an ongoing eschatological witness of the Spirit's work in this world. It is this one visible working of the Spirit that proves to be the witness of eschatological hope. Therefore, the present experience of speaking in tongues, like the tongues in Acts 2, reminds us of our current mission and our ultimate destiny.[49]

Without question, the outpouring of the Spirit at Pentecost created and sustained an eschatological perspective within the early church which caused them to viewed everything from within the framework of the imminent second coming of Christ.[50] Therefore, from a Pentecostal perspective, Pentecost was not the day the church began but rather the day the church got defined. The effect of Spirit baptism was that the church possessed a Spirit-directed understanding of its missional purpose and eschatological hope. It is this same Spirit-directed understanding of the church's purposes that drives Pentecostals to such intensity in prayer and praise (including speaking in tongues) and energizes their missional witness from within this one overarching purpose of eschatological hope. This interconnected, Spirit-directed passion for worship and mission flows out of eschatological hope, which is the root of Pentecostal theology and practice. Therefore, Spirit baptism (as evidenced by speaking in tongues) offers a unique

---

49. Menzies, *Speaking in Tongues*, 160.

50. Land, *Pentecostal Spirituality*, 55.

paradigm of eschatology that cannot help but reorientate all other frameworks of thinking.

Within a Pentecostal embracing of speaking in tongues, Spirit baptism not only offers a foretaste of the new Jerusalem but, in some real sense, offers a powerful testimony of eschatological realities in this present world. This actualization of eschatological power results in the Pentecostal seeing the world differently. Menzies explains:

> Speaking in tongues not only embodies and validates our reading of the bible, it also calls us to recognize who we are. It calls the church to recognize and remember its true identity. It reminds us that we are nothing less than a community of end-time prophets called and empowered to bear bold witness for Jesus.[51]

The Pentecostal sees eschatological themes not merely as some far-distant reality; rather, through glossolalia, we have the ability to participate in "signs and wonders" in this present age which point to an age to come. Moltmann suggests that it is exactly through the gifts of the Spirit that the Spirit exercises eschatological liberation to expand, diversify, and proliferate the many expressions of God's grace in this present world.[52] From this eschatological perspective, Pentecostals embrace a radical openness to God in this current age, with the understanding that this openness allows for a foretaste of our ultimate eschatological hope.

To the skeptic of speaking in tongues, the practice of speaking in tongues appears to be nothing more than an irrational, spiritual psychobabble of religious radicals. However, this mistaken approach fails to recognize that glossolalic speech communicates eschatological "groaning too deep for words" (Rom 8:26). The non-Pentecostal often fails to realize that Pentecostalism is far more than a "tongues movement"—that Pentecostalism is an eschatological movement at its core. Viewed within this light, the Pentecostal movement has done more than simply revive an emphasis on Spirit-baptism and charisma. It has helped to reorient the church to a more biblical eschatology.

---

51. Menzies, *Speaking in Tongues*, 3.
52. Moltmann, *Spirit of Life*, 45.

CONCLUSION

From the perspective of practical theology, speaking in tongues can be seen to have a powerful impact on the way in which Pentecostals live out their faith. Whether it is the way in which they communicate with God (prayer and praise), the way that they fulfill their purpose (mission), or the way they view the culmination of God's redemptive work (eschatology), speaking in tongues can be found to play an essential role in the practical theology of Pentecostalism.

With this understanding, Pentecostalism should recognize the value of guarding our distinction of speaking in tongues as more than protecting a novel doctrine. The move away from a theology and practice of speaking in tongues would not only significantly damage the distinct Pentecostal way of worship but would also drastically impact its missional, cultural, and eschatological philosophy. Like a string in a ball of yarn, the removal of speaking in tongues from Pentecostal doctrine would invariably affect Pentecostal practical theology in significant ways.

Since neither belief nor behavior functions independently, Pentecostals need to be sensitive to the fact that their biblical/theological approach to speaking in tongues will undoubtedly impact their practical theology. This means that any departure from the distinctive Pentecostal practice of speaking in tongues cannot be changed without significant ramifications. Therefore, Pentecostals would be wise to recognize the importance of holding to and continually reaffirming its distinct doctrine and practice of speaking in tongues as a means of preserving and defending their distinct practical theology.

4

A Social Science Perspective
of Speaking in Tongues

INTRODUCTION

The debate between science and Christian theology has continued to garner much attention in recent years. From questions surrounding the origins of the universe to whether or not science can speak to matters of ethics, the dialogue between science and religion has been vigorous. While Pentecostals have historically stayed away from involving themselves in this arena, there is a recent influx of scholars adding their voice to this discussion.[1] Speaking about the importance of Pentecostal engagement with the sciences, Pentecostal scholar Amos Yong writes, "As Pentecostals come to increasing realization that science has and will continue to shape their lives, I suggest that they can no longer put off critical engagement with it."[2] Therefore, to take seriously a multidisciplinarian examination of speaking in tongues, an examination of the phenomenon from within a social science perspective is necessary.

So important is a social science apologetic of speaking in tongues that it can be argued that if Pentecostals fail to defend its social science veracity, this failure could result in the eventual abandonment of its practice within the Pentecostal movement. That is to say, if a Pentecostal apologetic of speaking in tongues fails to engage with the social sciences, future

---

1. Most notably, the works of Pentecostal theologians Amos Yong and Frank Macchia.

2. Yong, "Academic Glossolalia?," 63.

generations will undoubtedly question or even disregard its practical validity as a means of prayer and praise to God.

If we take the Pentecostal distinctive of Spirit-inspired speaking in tongues seriously, we must not be afraid to examine the phenomenon from within a social science inquiry. If it is a biblically supported practice (which it clearly is), the Pentacostal should not fear whether the practice can stand up to scientific investigation. This is certainly not to say that the phenomenon of speaking in tongues can be primarily explained through the social sciences. Instead, the social sciences can allow Pentecostal's to possess a more comprehensive understanding of the nature of speaking in tongues.

SOCIOLOGICAL ASPECTS OF SPEAKING IN TONGUES

Over the last few decades, glossolalia—and by extension, Pentecostalism—has received an influx of attention from the social sciences due to its increase in acceptance within society. The practice of glossolalia has continued to entrench itself as a source of significant social importance within the church. So much so that speaking in tongues has transcended denominational lines to be practiced by many non-Pentecostal adherents. This has resulted in greater societal acceptance of speaking in tongues. It has moved from a fringe group at the margins of religious social groups to a prominent seat at the ecumenical table. In just over one hundred years, Pentecostalism has grown to be one of Christianity's most prominent and fastest-growing components.[3] As such, a modern Pentecostal contribution to academia must include an examination of speaking in tongues from within the social sciences.

Various forms of glossolalic practices could be studied from a sociological perspective (dramatic, pathological, pagan, etc.). For this study, the researcher will focus specifically on Christian speaking in tongues. With the rise of Pentecostalism, scholarly interest in the social influences of speaking in tongues has increased. Watson Mills, in his classic work *Speaking in Tongues: A Guide to Research on Glossolalia*, writes:

> The earliest examinations of glossolalia were centered almost exclusively in polemics. It was not until the debate about the usefulness of tongues subsided that researchers were motivated to put the phenomenon under the microscope and examine it as they would any other phenomenon in religious experience. The subject

3. Warrington, *Pentecostal Theology*, 1.

then became of interest to theologians, lexicographers, history of religionists, psychologists, sociologists, linguists, and behaviorists alike.[4]

Regrettably, early Pentecostal scholarship did not give much attention to the sociological aspects of speaking in tongues. Instead, the focus was primarily on defending the biblical fidelity of speaking in tongues. This is understandable given the fact that the opponents' attack against speaking in tongues was chiefly rooted in questions surrounding biblical exegesis or theological analysis. However, with the rise in popularity of Pentecostalism throughout the globe, the sociological impact of tongue speech has begun to gain the attention of many modern sociologists and religious scholars.

While Christian speaking in tongues can trace its roots back to the biblical account of the day of Pentecost in Acts, modern Pentecostals trace their roots back to the revivals in Topeka, Kansas, and Azusa Street in California in the early twentieth century. A historical analysis will reveal the myriad of sociocultural dynamics within Pentecostalism.[5] Even so, the central belief regarding the vitality and viability of speaking in other tongues has remained a primary tenant of Pentecostal faith and practice.

At the outset of the modern glossolalic phenomenon, many of its participants believed that their newfound language would provide for them the ability to go on the missionary field and speak a foreign language (*xenolalia*). The histories of these early Pentecostals reveal that these glossolalic adherents came home disappointed in their inability to speak in tongues and be understood by foreigners. In addressing the sociological impact of this embarrassment, Gary McGee writes:

> When the failure of tongues as a mission-linguistic tool became apparent, Pentecostals consequently retained their confidence in praying in tongues as the source of power, an approach both biblical and already familiar to them. Instead of this letdown traumatizing the self-understanding of the movement and blunting its growth, the fledgling diaspora of Pentecostal ministers and missionaries steadily increased decade after decade.[6]

Early Pentecostalism had its share of sociocultural mishaps as it sought to embrace the task of representing speaking in tongues within

4. Mills, *Theological/Exegetical Approach*, 12.
5. For a historical analysis of Pentecostalism, see Hollenweger, *Pentecostalism*.
6. McGee, "New World," 110.

society. It has nonetheless continued to thrive based upon the simple fact that Pentecostalism aims to promote more than a "religion of glossolalia"—it promotes life within the Spirit. This critical emphasis within early Pentecostalism has enabled speaking in tongues to withstand the many sociocultural attacks it has faced.

This was similar to the manner in which the onlooking crowd on the day of Pentecost assumed the glossolalic disciples were drunk (Acts 2:12–14). Modern Pentecostalism has encountered numerous mistaken assumptions regarding the sociocultural viability of speaking in tongues. Some have claimed that speaking in tongues is the result of some pathological disease.[7] Others maintain that it is the result of demonic possession,[8] or even that speaking in tongues is simply a form of regression speech equal to childish gibberish.[9] Despite the numerous attacks against the rationale of its practice, none of these charges have slowed its sociocultural advancement.

A historical analysis of the sociocultural environment of early Pentecostalism reveals that this movement arose among the marginalized of society. In his book *Thinking in the Spirit*, author Douglas Jacobson describes the sociological hurdles early Pentecostalism faced:

> Geographically, they came from all over the nation. But virtually none came from the ranks of the blue-blooded East Coast intellectual elite. If Pentecostals were going to make their voices heard in the larger society during the early years of the twentieth century, they were going to have to do it on their own. They had no high-culture coattails to ride to prominence.[10]

The sociocultural challenges facing early practitioners of speaking in tongues could have destroyed the phenomena had there not been something genuinely supernatural involved in its practice. From those described in biblical accounts in the New Testament to modern-day practicioners, the adherents of glossolalic experience have testified to the experience changing their lives by providing them with increased boldness in their faith.

---

7. For more information, see Osser et al., "Glossolalic Speech from a Psycholinguistic Perspective."

8. For more information, see MacArthur, *Strange Fire: The Danger of Offending the Holy Spirit with Counterfeit Worship.*

9. For more information, see Stagg et al., *Glossolalia: Tongue Speaking in Biblical, Historical, and Psychological Perspective.*

10. Jacobson, *Thinking in the Spirit*, x.

Although there is undeniable evidence suggesting that speaking in tongues (and by extension, Pentecostalism) has had a tremendous sociocultural impact, it would be a mistake to assume that sociocultural influences are the *cause* of glossolalic activity rather than the natural *consequence* of its supernatural appearance. Pattison writes about the noticeable sociocultural impact of Pentecostalism:

> There are many indications that the religious experiences involved in Pentecostalism increase the willingness to take risks . . . The experience of breaking with old religious patterns has been identified by many informants with a willingness to break with kinship, social, and economic patterns as well. To the degree that Pentecostalism increases self-confidence, inspires people to work and save, to cooperate, to take risks and accept innovation, and to break with old patterns, then it is indeed a religious motivation for sociocultural change and economic development.[11]

Because of the propensities described above, Pattison proposes that speaking in tongues is fundamentally a sociocultural learned behavior which is an accompaniment of a deep and significant spiritual experience. For Pattison, the meaning and function of tongue speech are closely tied to its sociocultural context. Thus, while its consequences may have deep and meaningful spiritual implications, "glossolalia per se is not a spiritual phenomenon."[12] Additionally, he argues that speaking in tongues is an experience that is available to anyone who is willing to adopt a submissive disposition concerning controlled speech and who has also been adequately supplied with the appropriate incentives within their social structures. However, since all human behavior can be classified as learned behavior, to say that the phenomenon of speaking in tongues can be explained only by pointing to learned behavior is really to say nothing about the subject at all—all forms of language are learned through some process of socialization. Therefore, Pattison's attempt to logically reject glossolalic activity on this basis would also require a rejection of all human languages as a valid form of communication.

A differentiation between aspects of speaking in tongues that can be attributed to learned behavior and the "ability" of the glossolalist to produce glossolalic utterance through learned behavior should be noted. To this point, William Samarin writes, "A person learns or can learn, a great deal

11. Pattison, "Behavioral Science Research," 81.
12. Pattison, "Behavioral Science Research," 86.

about the charismatic subculture, but he does not learn to talk in tongues."[13] While it is true that many glossolalists first experience glossolalic utterance within the context of a religious group, this is not always the case. In fact, Samarin records several instances of individuals whose first experience with speaking in tongues occurred with no prior knowledge of the phenomenon. Thus, while it is evident that sociocultural influences impact glossolalia speakers, to reduce the phenomenon of speaking in tongues to this point is to miss the multilayered spiritual aspects involved in the practice of speaking in tongues.

One straightforward way in which sociocultural influences drive learned behavior can be found in the worship service. The structure, emphasis, and expectations of a worship service can significantly impact sociocultural behavior. To this point, Virginia Hine explains:

> If speaking in tongues is "learned behavior" as suggested by many
> scholars, the decreased opportunity for public expression may be
> a main correlate for the decrease in tongue-speaking among many
> American sectors of the pentecostal/charismatic movements.[14]

Thus, while learned-behavior factors within sociocultural changes can influence glossolalic participation, it should not be assumed that these learned-behavior factors are the originators of the glossolalia phenomenon. Although speaking in tongues, in a general sense—like other spiritual events (salvation, water baptism, communion, etc.)—is influenced by learned behavior, this impact cannot fundamentally explain its existence.

Furthermore, evidence suggests that second-generation Pentecostals (those who have been socialized to accept speaking in tongues) speak in tongues less frequently than those who have come to the experience from denominations where the practice was either ignored or devalued.[15] In some cases, the more familiar participants are with speaking in tongues, the less frequently they practice speaking in tongues, despite their "advantageous" learned behavior. Therefore, to propose that the meaning and function of glossolalia results from learned behavior is a far too simplistic approach to the subject from both a spiritual and sociocultural perspective. Instead, a more comprehensive approach is warranted. The sociocultural influences

13. Samarin, "Glossolalia as Learned Behavior," 64.

14. Poloma, "Glossolalia," 155.

15. Hine, "Pentecostal Glossolalia," 212.

of speaking in tongues must be examined within the biblical context of prayer and praise to God.

Prayer and praise are, admittedly, influenced by sociocultural forces. However, for the person who practices these activities, it is evident that their functionality reaches beyond sociological descriptions. This is due to the fact that prayer and praise influence the spiritual dimensions of the human person. As such, although prayer and praise can be impacted by sociocultural forces, for the glossolalist, this does nothing to diminish their power or importance as viable spiritual practices. Mark Cartledge explains why:

> One of the obvious understandings gathered from the literature is that glossolalia is a prayer language that is used when the words of one's normal language prove inadequate. It transcends language and yet embodies language. It is a language of the spirit rather than of the mind, it is of the heart rather than the head. It functions as both a sign, as evidence of the presence of God in a special way, through the baptism of the Spirit, and as a gift of prayer in private and corporate settings. It can be a means of group identity and solidarity, a voice of the voiceless and the illiterate, as well as a release for those seeking freedom from the iron cage of grammar.[16]

As a mode of prayer and praise, speaking in tongues has the potential to change the individual who practices the phenomenon in a variety of significant ways. While speaking in tongues is not merely an isolated experience absent of any social implications, the glossolalic phenomena is simultaneously a spiritual activity that reaches beyond sociocultural stimuli to empower the glossolalist with a supernatural connection. Therefore, the tongues-speech phenomenon (as viewed within a biblical framework of prayer and praise) cannot simply be dismissed as a learned behavior because this explanation in no way invalidates its usage.

From a sociocultural perspective, when speaking in tongues is practiced, it has the potential to not only change the individual but also affect existing social norms and structures. Without question, speaking in tongues was a driving catalyst for the dynamic growth of Pentecostalism both within the United States and worldwide.[17] From its beginning, both biblically at Pentecost (Acts 2) and in modern Pentecostalism (Topeka and Azusa), Christian glossolalia had its origins not merely through sociological

16. Cartledge, *Charismatic Glossolalia*, 135.

17. For more information, see Anderson, *Introduction to Pentecostalism*.

forces but also through supernatural means. Therefore, while it cannot be denied that sociocultural influences have impacted both historical and modern glossolalic activity, these influences in and of themselves fail to offer a complete picture of glossolalic function.

Consequently, while a sociological framework does not provide a satisfactory explanation for glossolalia's origins, they do reveal that glossolalic activity can function within sociocultural norms. Samarin discusses the variables and variations of glossolalic activity within society:

> When we look at the culture of the glossolalist, we find no reason to judge him abnormal. Like other Christians, he believes that the Holy Spirit dwells in him and motivates him. The only difference is in the manner in which Pentecostals differ on the manifestation of the Spirit and how this presence is manifested physically through the baptized person.[18]

As such, the practice of glossolalia should not be assumed to be the result of sociological abnormalities which can explain the glossolalist's experience.

In fact, Hine's research revealed that glossolalic adherents possessed vast differences in socioeconomic, educational, and church backgrounds. Furthermore, the study found the primary sociocultural connection between glossolalists was that 91 percent attended church regularly even before conversion to Pentecostalism.[19] Thus, one apparent sociocultural predisposition to speaking in tongues is that their religious worldview infuses a great sense of meaning. Coupled with recent research that strongly supports the fact that religious belief and practice significantly improves self-esteem, life satisfaction, ability to handle stress, and overall physical health, as a mode of spiritual prayer and praise, the phenomenon of speaking in tongues can be viewed as within the boundaries of social norms.[20]

LINGUISTIC ASPECTS OF SPEAKING IN TONGUES

With the rise in cultural influence, Pentecostalism has also warranted an increased scholarly interest in the linguistic nature of speaking in tongues. Those who have studied the linguistic aspects of speaking in tongues have

18. Samarin, "Variation and Variables," 123.
19. Hine, "Pentecostal Glossolalia," 223.
20. Ellison, "Religious Involvement," 83.

typically concluded that while the phenomenon displays traces of natural languages, it ultimately cannot meet the criteria due to its deficiency of any convincing quality of semanticity.[21] In his linguistic study of speaking in tongues, William Samarian defines the phenomenon as "unintelligible extemporaneous post-babbling speech that exhibits superficially phonologic similarity to language without having consistent syntagmatic structure and that is not systematically derived from or related to a known language."[22] However, studying the linguistic aspects of glossolalia from only a semantic perspective fails to evaluate the complete nature of the "words" being used within glossolalic speech.

Since biblically, speaking in tongues is first and foremost prayer and praise to God, limiting a linguistic study of the phenomenon to the "words" being uttered fails to reach the heart of the act being performed. This would be the same mistake that could be made if the linguistic characteristics of any prayer or praise were examined in a known language simply for their linguistic properties. Doing so would assume that since the linguistic aspects of the words are understood, this can account for all the action being done. Sacramental elements of prayer and praise communicate ideas and meanings beyond the limits of a linguistic examination of the words spoken. Therefore, the "words" spoken in prayer and praise reach far beyond their semantic nature and communicate something of our being.

While some modern researchers have continued to search for a neurological link within the linguistic mechanisms of speaking in tongues,[23] none have been able to explain the nature of the phenomenon. However, a recent development in the philosophy of language aids our understanding of the ways in which glossolalic activity can be seen as a means of communication. J. L. Austin[24] and John Searle[25] established a groundbreaking linguistic work called speech act theory of language. This theory claims that language is a medium through which some action happens, since words are vehicles that *do* things.[26] Because this framework for language appreciates what language does, it allows for expressions that have no words yet do

21. See Samarin, *Men and Angels*; and Motley, "Linguistic Analysis of Glossolalia."

22. Samarin, "Variation and Variables," 123.

23. See Kéri et al., "Learning in Glossolalia"; and Walter, "Brain Structural Evidence."

24. Austin, *How to Do Things*.

25. Searle, *Speech Acts*.

26. See Bartholomew et al., *After Pentecost* for an exhaustive look at the importance of speech-act theory within linguistic issues of biblical interpretation.

something of communicative nature. James K. A. Smith elaborates on this point:

> Speech act theory provides a unique account of the way language *works*—or more specifically, that language is a realm of action that does work beyond the narrow task of conveying ideas from one mind to another. As such, it also does justice to the pluriform ways that language functions in different contexts and for different interests.[27]

Suppose we understand the primary function of language to be that of *doing* something. In that case, it is logical to postulate glossolalic activity as *doing* a communicative function within the practitioner's life. Furthermore, since from a biblical perspective speaking in tongues functions as prayer and praise, it is apparent that the practitioner is doing something with significant communicative qualities in the act of tongue speech. Linguists such as William Samarin and Michael T. Motely have concluded that speaking in tongues is, at its best, pseudo-linguistic. Yet, if speaking in tongues can be shown to have communicative properties, then it becomes a language that does linguistic action. While glossolalic speech may have an unsemantic nature, when viewed through a biblical understanding of speaking in tongues as a spiritual act of prayer and praise, it is clear the phenomenon functions as a communicative act.

In the act of glossolalic speech, the pray-er is doing an act that is expressing something to God in what Paul described as "groanings too deep for words" (Rom 8:26). While glossolalic praying is not intended to communicate propositional information, supposing that this mode of praying does not qualify as an act of *doing* prayer is to restrict the definition of prayer significantly. Instead, glossolalic prayer frees the pray-er up to be receptive to the Spirit's working in their prayer and enables them to intercede in situations when "we do not know how to pray as we should" (Rom 8:26). Since human limitations inhibit even the act of prayer, speaking in tongues enables the person who prays to go beyond the human confines of language to communicate with God through the Spirit. In explaining the fact that glossolalic prayer goes beyond human understanding, Paul says, "For if I pray in tongue, my spirit prays but my mind is unfruitful. What am I to do? I will pray with my spirit, but I will pray with my mind also;" (1 Cor 14:13–15). Given the human limitations inherent in *doing* communicative acts with God, speaking in tongues provides the pray-er with a mode

27. Smith, "Tongues as Resistance Discourse," 83.

of linguistic expression that is not limited by the rules of standard human language.

Likewise, the act of *doing* speaking in tongues can function as praise to God. When the Spirit was poured out at Pentecost, the gathered crowd exclaimed, "We hear them telling in our own tongues the mighty works of God" (Acts 2:11). Clearly, the result of this Spirit-inspired tongue speech was that these Jews heard the disciples speaking praises to God in their native languages. Therefore, if we consider that speaking in tongues can also function as *xenolalia* (as in the case of Acts 2), then an undeniable case can be made that speaking in tongues can operate as communicative speech.[28] On the day of Pentecost, we find that the first ecumenical language of the church was not Hebrew, Greek, or Latin; rather, through glossolalic speech, "every language under heaven" (Acts 2:5) was included in the outpouring of Spirit baptism.

The phenomenon of speaking in tongues at Pentecost produced a clear gospel witness that offered praise to God and was readily understood and received by the crowd. Like prayer, the spiritual act of praising God is bound by human limitations. Therefore, glossolalic praise enables the one praising—through the Spirit—to go beyond the finite confines of natural language and praise God. Paul continues his explanation of this glossolalic function by saying, "I will sing praise with my spirit, but I will sing with my mind also" (1 Cor 14:15). Thus, just as with prayer, the act of glossolalic praise enables the praiser to *do* communication and expression toward God, which expresses a depth of praise that is uninhibited by the restrictive rules of human language.

Additionally, Paul notes that speaking in tongues, which occurs within a religious context, should communicate a clear sign of God's presence to unbelievers (1 Cor 14:22). The classification of divine "signs and wonders" is not limited to prophetic words but also includes symbolic instruments such as fire, wind, and sounds, as in the case of the Spirit's arrival at Pentecost (Acts 2). These "signs and wonders," although having no human linguistic qualities, still provide a mode of expression which attests to the divine reality of Spirit's indwelling. Additionally, it is evident that a Pauline theology of speaking in tongues views the phenomenon as a clear act of communication. For this reason, Paul warned the Corinthian church against glossolalic activity within the congregation that does not result in

---

28. For documented accounts of modern *xenolalia* taking place, see May, *Global Witness to Pentecost*.

an interpretation, making the primary goal of glossolalic activity to be that of communicative action (1 Cor 14:22–25).

As a communicative action, the physical act of speaking in tongues is not merely a symbol of spiritual activity but is in itself the presentation of Spirit-directed action. Under the inspiration of the Spirit, glossolalic speech provides a beautiful union of human-divine communication, as the practitioner is speaking yet at the same time yielding and surrendering their speech. To this point, Murray Dempster remarks:

> The Spirit's power to incorporate a group's participation in the creative remaking of language was a sign that portended the Spirit's power to initiate a group's participation in the creative remaking of history.[29]

From this perspective, speaking in tongues provides humanity with a powerful communicative reunification to divine life that serves in two crucial ways. First, the linguistic action of glossolalic speech facilitates a transcendent utterance that enables divine empowerment. In other words, the act of glossolalic prayer and praise causes the practitioner to *do* communicative action, which the Spirit inspires. The result of this divinely inspired action is the empowerment of the practitioner as their physical vessel is infused with the life of the Spirit. No more clear picture of this can be found than on the day of Pentecost, when the Spirit transformed a weak human vessel (Peter's mouth) into a veritable oracle of God to communicate Spirit-inspired speech. Through the unique act of glossolalic speech, the disciples' entire beings were transformed into messengers of divine revelation. This transformation took place in fulfillment of Christ's prophecy concerning the arrival of Spirit baptism, which would transform them into witnessing *beings* (Acts 1:8). The extraordinary transformation which takes place at Spirit baptism is realized through the communicative unification of human and divine utterances within glossolalic speech. For this reason, the act of glossolalic speech serves as a physical sign of Spirit baptism to mark the divine-human paradigm shift within our beings. Through glossolalic "words," we communicate the reality that the divine-human relationship has been infused with a reality too great for words (1 Cor 14:2).

Secondly, glossolalic speech provides us with an eschatological pointer to a recreative reality of redemptive history that is yet to come (Rev 7:9). As a kind of reversal of Babel, glossolalia serves to reunify the languages of

---

29. Dempster, "Church's Moral Witness," 6.

humanity within a "heavenly" language designed to offer prayer and praise to God. The divine design for human worship was that all of humanity be united in our language of worship. Yet, the human heart has been divided into a thousand idols of worship because of man's rebellious sin. However, the act of glossolalic prayer and praise offers both a present reunification of humanity's worship and an eschatological foretaste into a future age that is yet to be realized. Therefore, participating in glossolalic speech is to participate in an eschatological yearning to unify all things (including language) into God's kingdom. Speaking in tongues enhances our human/spiritual existences because it connects us to God's presence on a deeper level than our limited cognitive or linguistic capabilities. As such, tongues push the boundaries of human speech to capture and express the mystery of God's redemptive presence in the midst of this present age.

While the formal linguistic analysis of speaking in tongues has offered little in explaining the nature of the phenomenon, seen within a biblical framework of prayer and praise to God, the act of speaking in tongues is clearly doing a communicative function. Beyond a mere symbol of religious speech, speaking in tongues is in itself the embodiment of Spirit-directed action since it unites human-divine communication. This unification of human-divine speech allows for the life of the Spirit to empower human beings and offers a glimpse into our eschatological hope.

PSYCHOLOGICAL ASPECTS OF SPEAKING IN TONGUES

The psychological aspects of speaking in tongues have long been of interest to scientists who have sought to understand the phenomenon's underlying mental and emotional significance. In the late nineteenth century William James (1842–1910) helped to popularize the study of psychology. As the father of American psychology, his work and theories laid the foundation for psychological research. His definition of psychology as "the science of mental life" legitimized psychology as a scientific field of study.[30] Building upon James' work, the neurologist Sigmund Freud (1856–1939) popularized the field of psychoanalysis as a means of treating various psychopathologies. Freud interpreted religious experience from a purely naturalistic perspective. Thus, in a Freudian evaluation, anyone who claimed a religious experience like speaking in tongues would have been immediately classified as

30. See Evans, "Principles of Psychology."

having a mental disorder.[31] The origins of these scientific fields are significant because they coincide with the beginnings of the modern Pentecostal movement. Starting from the events in Topeka, Kansas, in 1901, the Azusa Street revival in 1906, and the creation of the Assemblies of God in 1916, Pentecostalism came into existence at almost the same time as the modern scientific disciplines of psychology and psychiatry.

An examination of early studies on speaking in tongues shows that the researchers viewed glossolalic activity as a pathological abnormality. Alexander Mackie explained speaking in tongues as the result of psychotic instabilities brought on by an unstable nervous system that was prone to hyper-emotionalism.[32] G. B. Cutten proposed that glossolalic behavior was psychologically related to hysteria and schizophrenia.[33] These psychologists, among many others, reacted to the emerging Pentecostal phenomenon of speaking in tongues by categorizing the activity as the result of a variety of psychological disorders. The majority of these early psychologists who researched glossolalic activity either associated it with theories of psychological regression and narcissism or studied whether or not the glossolalic behavior served to disintegrate or integrate the personality of the practitioner. However, the problem with these modes of research was that they came tainted with the assumption that glossolalic activity is abnormal. Despite these early opponents of speaking in tongues, subsequent research has revealed a very different perspective on the psychological state of practitioners.

One of the first to theorize that glossolalia could have positive psychological value was the French psychologist Emile Lombard. In 1910, Lombard proposed that even if glossolalia could be defined as regressive speech, it could still have psychological value within a meaningful religious experience. Lombard found that speaking in tongues has psychological value in that it illuminates piety and passionate love for God.[34] Significantly, Lombard recognized the potential psychological importance of speaking in tongues at such an early period. This contribution opened the door for later researchers to contemplate the possible benefits of the phenomenon, even though such a difference of opinion existed as to whether tongue speech should be classified as aberrant or positive behavior.

31. Kay, "Mind, Behavior, and Glossolalia."
32. See Mackie, *Gift of Tongues*, 82.
33. See Cutten, *Speaking with Tongues*, 158.
34. For more information, see Lombard, *Glossolalie*, 110.

For example, after examining the psychological impact of religious glossolalia on the personality of practitioners, A. A. Lovekin concluded the following:

> This phenomenon is not, therefore, pathological nor infantile. It can free the conscious mind from its extreme rationalism. It can allow the emotional life of the psyche not only a means of expression but also a method of nurture. Speaking with tongues can be a most concrete means of expressing joy and praise to God. It is a genuine witness to the presence of the Holy Spirit in one's life.[35]

For Lovekin, it was not only possible for speaking in tongues to have a positive psychological impact, but glossolalia served as a legitimate witness of the working of the Spirit.

Through a cross-cultural study of glossolalia, Goodman concluded that to assume within a psychoanalytic study that glossolalic activity is linked to hysteria or schizophrenia is an error because this conclusion is not supported by empirical evidence.[36] Likewise, Osser, Ostwald, MacWhinney, and Casey concluded that glossolalic behavior could only be considered pathological if used in a nonreligious context for the purpose of confusing the listener.[37] Therefore, from the biblical framework of speaking in tongues as prayer and praise to God, the phenomenon cannot be classified as psychologically aberrant behavior.

John Kildahl argues that a psychological preoccupation with inner needs seems to provide an essential condition for a person to begin speaking in tongues. He assumes that the tongue speaker loses all or part of their locus of control during the glossolalic process. However, even with the assumption that ego control is somehow suspended, in his book *The Psychology of Speaking in Other Tongues,* he states:

> Perhaps the most significant finding of this research is that one group is not any more mentally healthy than the other. On any broad criteria of emotional well-being, the tongue-speakers and non-tongue-speakers were about the same.[38]

Furthermore, Kildahl's assumption that there is temporary regression of the locus of control during glossolalic activity has been found to be wrong.

---

35. Lovekin, "Glossolalia," 129.
36. Goodman, *Speaking in Tongues,* 82.
37. Osser et al., "Glossolalic Speech," 19.
38. Kildahl, *Speaking in Tongues,* 48.

Coulson and Johnson found that tongue speakers exhibited a greater internal locus of control than non-tongue-speakers.[39] Coulson addresses the results of this study:

> Stereotypical thinking about the glossolalist, suggesting emotional illness, suggestibility, powerlessness, low I.Q., and low socioeconomic status needs to be discarded, or at least reconsidered. He is very much like other Christians yet varies from them in his approach to some of his activities. It would appear that these people should be looked at, not as a pathological person, but rather as people who have found for themselves a lifestyle that explains their existence.[40]

Thus, contrary to earlier research, glossolalists do not suffer from an aberrant psychological disorder or show more significant signs of psychopathology. Neither are they more susceptible to hypnosis or neurotic behavior or primarily dependent on authority figures.[41] While the early psychological research on speaking in tongues was clearly negatively biased and laden with prejudicial tendencies, contemporary research has revealed that speaking in tongues performed within a meaningful religious context can occur within psychologically healthy people.

CONCLUSION

This chapter has provided an examination of the social science aspects of the subject of speaking in tongues. Having observed recent research on the subject of glossolalia from a sociological, linguistic, and psychological perspective, it is evident that speaking in tongues performed within the religious framework of prayer and praise to God can be viewed as normative behavior. Whether sociologically, linguistically, or psychologically, an analysis of speaking in tongues reveals that the phenomenon functions consistently within a biblical framework of sacramental prayer and praise to God. Sociologically, the act of speaking in tongues brings fellowship with other believers who practice the phenomenon of speaking in tongues in Spirit-directed ways. Linguistically, speaking in tongues enables the believer to communicate with God in ways that stretch the boundaries of human

---

39. Coulson and Johnson, "Glossolalia," 317.
40. Coulson and Johnson, "Glossolalia," 316.
41. Kay, "Mind, Behavior, and Glossolalia," 204.

language and declare his wonders. And psychologically, the glossolalist is able to express their innermost feelings in prayer and praise to God. Therefore, speaking in tongues serves as a biblical sacrament that strengthens the spiritual dimension of human existence in its quest to communicate with God.

5

A Historical Perspective
of Speaking in Tongues

INTRODUCTION

In beginning a historical analysis of speaking in tongues, it is essential to note that this phenomenon is not unique to Christianity. This fact may come as a surprise to some, but descriptions of ecstatic speech are found within a comparative study of other religions. In some cases, the events of non-Christian glossolalic activity have a striking resemblance to the glossolalic speech described in the New Testament.[1] So the question must be asked: Does the fact that pagan worshipers have historically practiced glossolalic utterances undermine the Christian practice? The cessationist would point to the pagan practice of glossolalia as a sign that the practice is demonic.[2] However, the fact that pagan religions have utilized glossolalic speech in their worship of false gods should no more serve to invalidate its practice within Christendom than the fact that pagan religions have used songs and instruments in their worship of false gods. In other words, the fact that a pagan religion implements the use of a particular practice in its religious tradition does nothing to diminish the use of that same practice in worship of the one true God. The only caveat to this must be the obvious foundation that as Christians, our modes of worship are influenced and guided by the sacred Scriptures. Therefore, for the Christian, whether a particular mode of worship can also be found to be used within a pagan context does not

1. Bromiley, *Standard Bible Encyclopedia*, 4:874.
2. John MacArthur makes this claim in his book *Strange Fire*, 150.

matter in the least. The only concern for the Christian should be whether the practice has support from within Scripture.

To this point, we have already shown extensively that speaking in tongues is found to be a normative practice within the early church. Furthermore, there is undeniable evidence that the apostle Paul practiced speaking in tongues as a mode of divine communication (1 Cor 4:14–18). As such, it is evident that regardless of any pagan association with the phenomenon prior to the early church, that association did nothing to invalidate the practice in the mind of the apostle Paul. Even if one wants to argue that speaking in tongues is somehow a "wholly" pagan practice, a New Testament theology of worship recognizes that false gods and their worship are to have no power over the way in which we worship God (1 Cor 8). Just as God was able to sanctify the pagan practice of offering meat to idols (1 Cor 8:8) in order that it could now provide sanctifying strength to the physical life of the Christian, so God is able to also sanctify the practice of speaking in tongues so that it can provide power to the spiritual life of the Christian. The fact that speaking in tongues has a historical association with pagan worship fails to discredit its clear acceptance in a New Testament context of believers.

CHARISMA DURING THE PATRISTIC PERIOD

At the center of the debate regarding the validity of speaking in tongues is the question of whether the gift of tongues ceased following the apostle's ministry. From a cessationist perspective, the argument is made that tongue speech ceased sometime after the last apostle's death. To validate this point, many cessationists point to church history as a validating proof for this argument. And while the evidence reveals an undeniable change in charismatic activity, the evidence also supports a Pentecostal understanding that contends that the charismatic gifts only declined after the early church and continued to be in use throughout church history in various places.

Additionally, it must be pointed out that it is an a priori assumption of modern historians that historical silence on a particular subject denotes its absence. It can just as easily be argued that historical silence on a subject is due to the fact that it was such a normative practice of that period that it needed no explanation.[3] Given the fact that most patristic writings are constructed in order to offer an apologetic defense against some heretical

3. Hunter, "Tongues-Speech," 136.

doctrine, it seems logical to conclude that if speaking in tongues was viewed as heretical, it would have been addressed. Instead, the evidence suggests that the decline of charismatic gifts was more sociological than theological, due to the fact that the church was undergoing significant cultural changes.[4] It should go without saying that a sociological shift within a particular period of church history does nothing to rule out any biblically established theological position.

Thus, a Pentecostal position on spiritual charisma maintains that even if speaking in tongues or other charismatic activity did completely cease after the last apostle's death, this failure of succeeding generations to utilize charisma does nothing to negate Pentecostalism's insistence that there is biblical evidence supporting its use. Since there is nothing within Scripture that would hint at the idea that charismatic empowerment should cease at the end of the apostolic period, it should be concluded that charismatic activity should continue to function within the church throughout the entirety of the church age. Furthermore, it should be pointed out that there is no biblical support for the idea that these charismatic gifts were primarily for the *apostles*. Instead, it is evident that charismatic giftings were designed primarily for the *church*. The cessationist position that charismatic gifts ceased after the apostles died presupposes that charisma was only *for* the apostles. This is a false assumption that has no foundation in Scripture. Instead, a biblical perspective of charisma recognizes that God gave it to the church to empower its witness throughout the entirety of the church age. This position can be supported by a careful examination of the early church fathers and what they wrote about spiritual manifestations.

The first non-apostle to speak favorably about charismatic gifts was Clement of Rome (35–99 AD). The first pope of Rome, Clement, writing to the church at Corinth, states:

> Thus a deep and luxurious peace was given to all, an insatiable desire for good deeds, and a full outpouring of the Holy Spirit was upon all of you. And filled with holy plans, in great eagerness with pious confidence, you stretched your hands to the Almighty God.[5]

It should be noted that much like the apostles' letters, the writings of the apostolic fathers within the patristic period focus primarily on an orientation

---

4. Ash "Decline of Ecstatic Prophecy," 241.

5. Brannan, *Apostolic Fathers*, 12.

of pastoral function and not a theological orientation.[6] For in this writing, the main appeal is for obedience, faith, piety, and hospitality within the church. Clement calls the Corinthian church to humility and peace and the pursuit of a holy life.[7] However, within the limited number of historical writings of this period, there are hints that this period had charismatic activity as the church grew.

Another example of this can be found in the writings of Ignatius of Antioch (c. 110 AD). As one of the earliest bishops in the history of the church, Saint Ignatius often speaks of the working of charismatic gifts in his writings.[8] The bishop of Antioch, Saint Ignatius was highly influential as a church leader and theologian in the era of history right after the apostolic period. The seven letters written by Ignatius serve as a warning against false doctrines and false teachers that were prevalent in this period.

Like Clement, Ignatius was concerned with preserving a variety of early Christian creeds that were the confessional practices of many early churches.[9] Writing to Polycarp of Smyrna, another bishop, Ignatius encourages Polycarp to:

> Be wise like the serpent in all things, and always innocent like the dove. For this reason you are physical and spiritual, so that you may deal graciously with whatever is visible before your face; and ask that the invisible be revealed to you, so that you may lack nothing and you may abound in every gift.[10]

From Ignatius's letters, we find supportive statements of the everyday use of spiritual gifts within the church during this period. Additionally, in Ignatius's letters to the churches of Ephesus, Magnesia, Tralles, Rome, Philadelphia, and Smyrna, there is evidence that this early church leader encouraged these congregations to be Spirit empowered in their stand against wickedness.

An additional example of charisma being practiced within the patristic period can be found in *The Shepherd of Hermas* document. While the exact date of this work is unknown, it is commonly associated with a date

6. Hunter, "Tongues-Speech," 125.

7. Jefford, *Apostolic Fathers*, 12.

8. Brennan, *Apostolic Fathers*, 79, 86, 117, 106 ("Ignatius to the Ephesians" 17:2, "Ignatius to the Magnesians" 8:2, "Ignatius to the Smyrnaeans" 9:2, "Ignatius to Polycarp" 2:2).

9. Jefford, *Apostolic Fathers*, 16.

10. Brennan, *Apostolic Fathers*, 117.

somewhere between the late second century and early third century. Made up of a collection of parables, poems, and apocalyptic pictures, *The Shepherd of Hermas* offers an interesting testimony of the perspective of this period. For our purposes, one of the most interesting passages is found in *Hermas* 43:9, which states:

> Therefore when the person who has the divine spirit comes into the assembly of righteous men who have the faith of the divine spirit, and intercession is made to God by the assembly of those men, then the angel of the prophetic spirit who rests on him, he fills the person, and being filled, the person with the Holy Spirit speaks to the group just as the Lord desires. Therefore thus will the divine spirit be evident.[11]

From these comments, it is evident that charismatic activity within the church during this period was not unknown. What is seen described within *The Shepherd of Hermas* is undeniably something very similar to what the apostle Paul lays out for the proper use of charismatic prophecy.

Additionally, Justin Martyr (c. 160 AD), the early church philosopher and defender of the Christian faith, offers a written testament of the active role of charisma in the patristic period. In his *Dialogue with Trypho*, he writes:

> Knowing that daily some [of you] are becoming disciples in the name of Christ, and quitting the path of error; who are also receiving gifts, each as he is worthy, illumined through the name of this Christ. For one receives the spirit of understanding, another of counsel, another of strength, another of healing, another of foreknowledge, another of teaching, and another of the fear of God.[12]

While it is fascinating to compare Justin Martyr's list of charisma with that of the apostle Paul, what is without debate is that they both describe the same thing—charismatic gifts operating within the church. In response to this clear affirmation of charismatic gifts working within the church, Trypho suggests that Justin Martyr is crazy for holding these sentiments. However, Justin Martyr responds by stating:

> Listen, O friend, I am not mad or beside myself; but it was prophesied that, after the ascent of Christ to heaven, He would deliver us from error and give us gifts. The words are these: He ascended

11. Brannan, *Apostolic Fathers*, 204.

12. Martyr, *Dialogue with Trypho*, 44.

up on high; He led captivity captive; He gave gifts to men. Accordingly, we who have received gifts from Christ, who has ascended up on high, prove from the words of prophecy that you, the wise in yourselves, and the men of understanding in your own eyes, are foolish, and honour God and His Christ by lip only. But we, who are instructed in the whole truth, honour Them both in acts, and in knowledge, and in heart, even unto death.[13]

Justin Martyr's unabashed support of charisma is clear evidence of the fact that their operation within the church did not cease after the death of the apostles. Furthermore, this interaction between Martyr and Trypho reveals that false teachers were attacking charisma even from this early period. This understanding should encourage the modern Pentecostal to stand up to current-day cessationism's false teaching.

Later in *Dialogue with Trypho*, Justin Martyr again affirms the presence of charisma and defends its use by stating:

For the prophetical gifts remain with us, even to the present time. And hence you ought to understand that the gifts formerly among your nation (Jews) have been transferred to us. And just as there were false prophets contemporaneous with your holy prophets, so are there now many false teachers amongst us, of whom our Lord forewarned us to beware; so that in no respect are we deficient, since we know that He foreknew all that would happen to us after His resurrection from the dead and ascension to heaven. For He said we would be put to death, and hated for His name's sake; and that many false prophets and false Christs would appear in His name, and deceive many: and so has it come about. For many have taught godless, blasphemous, and unholy doctrines, forging them in His name; have taught, too, and even yet are teaching, those things which proceed from the unclean spirit of the devil, and which were put into their hearts. Therefore we are most anxious that you be persuaded not to be misled by such persons.[14]

This powerful defense of charisma within the patristic period by Justin Martyr should stir every Pentecostal to continue to proclaim a bold witness to the necessity of charisma within the church in our day. The evidence is overwhelming from Justin's *Dialogue with Trypho* that Christians of this period were, in fact, no strangers to the activity of charisma within

---

13. Martyr, *Dialogue with Trypho*, 45.

14. Justin Martyr, *Dialogue with Trypho*, 99.

the church.[15] Furthermore, it demonstrates that this biblically supported activity was already under attack by false teachers.

Another historical figure from this period that must be examined is Irenaeus of Lyons (130–202 AD). Perhaps his most famous statement, which speaks in favor of charismatic gifts and possibly even alludes to speaking in tongues, can be found in his treatise on false teachings, entitled *Against Heresies*, where he writes:

> For this reason does the apostle declare, "We speak wisdom among them that are perfect," terming those persons "perfect" who have received the Spirit of God, and who through the Spirit of God do speak in all languages, as he used Himself also to speak. In like manner we do also hear many brethren in the church, who possess prophetic gifts, and who through the Spirit speak all kinds of languages, and bring to light for the general benefit the hidden things of men and declare the mysteries of God, whom also the apostle terms "spiritual," they being spiritual because they partake of the Spirit.[16]

Whether or not this is a reference to glossolalic utterance can be debated, but what is clear is that Irenaeus believed in the use of charisma within the church. Additionaly, in response to the heretic Marcion of Sinope, Irenaeus says:

> And others do not admit the gifts of the Holy Spirit, and reject from themselves the charism of Prophecy, being watered whereby, man bears fruit of life to God. And those are the ones spoken of by Isaias; for they shall be, he says, as a leafless terebinth and as a garden without water. And such men are of no use to God, in that stye can bear no fruit.[17]

There can be no question as to the fact that Irenaeus believed in the continuation of the gifts of the Spirit and defended the church against those who would seek to minimize the importance of charismatic workings in the lives of believers.

A contemporary of Irenaeus who also strongly supported the continuation of charismatic gifts was Tertullian (155–220 AD). The writings of Tertullian contain more references and allusions to charisma than any other early Christian writer. So strongly does Tertullian believe in the active

15. Kydd, *Charismatic Gifts*, 592.

16. Irenaeus, *Against Heresies*, 518.

17. Ash, "Decline of Ecstatic Prophecy," 249.

working of spiritual gifts that in his five-volume work *Against Marcion*, his primary defense against the heretical teaching of Marcion is that Marcion can offer no evidence of any spiritual gifts begin produced by his false god:

> [Tertullian challenged Marcion to] exhibit, as gifts of his god, some prophets, such as have not spoken by human sense, but with the Spirit of God . . . ; let him produce a psalm, a vision, a prayer—only let it be by the Spirit, in an ecstasy, that is, in a rapture, whenever an interpretation of tongues has occurred to him . . . . Now all these signs (of spiritual gifts) are forthcoming from my side without any difficulty.[18]

It was from the continuation of spiritual gifts that Tertullian based his apologetic argument against Marcion's dual-gods heresy. The fact that Tertuallian used spiritual gifts as a defense against false doctrines should underscore their importance in the church during the patristic period. In revealing Tertullian's thought process concerning the grounds for which spiritual gifts operate within the church, Ronald Kydd points to several important passages in the *De anima*. He states:

> Tertullian thinks his community had become eligible for prophesy because we acknowledge the spiritual gifts. Prophecy could occur because they believed that spiritual gifts were important and that they were in the church. A little later he implies that no one should be surprised at this, because this is exactly the way the Apostle Paul had said it would be.[19]

Another critical passage from the writings of Tertullian that indicates his support for the continuation of spiritual gifts can be found in his treatise *Concerning Baptism*. At the conclusion of this work, Tertullian writes:

> Therefore, blessed ones, whom the grace of God awaits, when you ascend from that most sacred font of your new birth, and spread your hands for the first time in the house of your mother, together with your brethren, ask from the Father, ask from the Lord, that His own specialties of grace and distributions of gifts may be supplied you. "Ask," says He, "and you shall receive." Well, you have asked, and have received; you have knocked, and it has been opened to you.[20]

---

18. Roberts and Donaldson, *Tertullianus against Marcion*, 411.

19. Kydd, *Charismatic Gifts*, 89.

20. Roberts and Donaldson, *Writings of Tertullian*, 256.

The fact that Tertullian encourages newly baptized converts that they should expect to receive spiritual gifts reveals that charismatic activity was not some rare or novel activity but was the normative pattern of the Christian community at this time.

One final example of charisma within the patristic period can be seen in Hilary of Poitiers (310–67 AD). In his work *On the Trinity*, he writes:

> Learn how these members which minister are also members which work, when he says, You are the body of Christ, and of Him members indeed. For God has set some in the church, first apostles, in whom is the word of wisdom; secondly prophets, in whom is the gift of knowledge; thirdly teachers, in whom is the doctrine of faith; next mighty works, among which are the healing of diseases, the power to help, governments by the prophets, and gifts of either speaking or interpreting various kinds of tongues. Clearly these are the church's agents of ministry and work of whom the body of Christ consists; and God has ordained them.[21]

It is evident that Hilary of Poitiers viewed charisma as a valid operation within the church for the edification of the entire body. This understanding aligns perfectly with a Pauline understanding of charismatic gifts and their function within the church. From this extensive listing of charisms, it is clear that the author intended to protect and foster charismatic gifts within the local church.[22]

It is also significant that Hilary mentions speaking in tongues and the interpretation of tongues within his list of God's ordained charisma. Four times in his formal treatise on the Trinity, Hilary of Poitiers records the entirety of the apostle Paul's list of spiritual gifts and includes tongues in the list every time. Whether or not Hilary of Poitiers practiced speaking in tongues is unknown, but what is evident from his writings is the fact that he was fully committed to their efficacy in his day. While many cessationists argue that speaking in tongues was a momentary spiritual gift that ceased with the death of the last apostle, the testimony of Hilary of Poitiers offers a clear contrast to this position. Writing some two hundred years after the final apostle's death, Hilary's treatise *On the Trinity* offers clear evidence that speaking in tongues was still active within the church.

A careful reading of this patristic period reveals a church that supports the use of charisma within the local assembly of believers. Given the

---

21. Hilary of Poitiers, *On the Trinity*, 147.
22. Williams and Waldvogel, "History," 61.

vast amount of writing during this period on the use of charismatic gifts within the church, what should be made of the fact of the infrequency of glossolalia? Many scholars have come to two conclusions on this matter: Cessationists have used this to claim that glossolalic gifts ceased. In contrast, Pentecostal academics have argued that charismatic gifts were so commonplace that they deserved little discussion.[23] If the cessationist perspective concerning speaking in tongues were correct, it would seem that the entirety of spiritual gifts would have ceased and not just speaking in tongues. Since it is clear that there was not a complete ceasing of charismatic gifts in the patristic period, it would seem logical that the Pentecostal perspective on the matter is more accurate.

So, if these early church fathers believed in charisma, what happened to cause the decline of their use within the church? The answer lies in the fact that the church began to become very institutionalized after this period. In response to the Montanist crisis, the institutional church began to reject the use of charisma. Through the closing of the biblical canon of Scripture, they also sought to close the operation of charisma. The ecstatic excesses of the Montanists gave license for a rejection of charisma not on biblical grounds but based on "rationalistic" objections. To this point, Ash writes:

> The theological basis for Christian prophecy, the Pauline charismata, continued to be espoused by orthodoxy despite so serious a threat as the Montanist enthusiasm. If ecstatic prophecy was never ruled out theologically, then we must look elsewhere to find explanations for its decline.[24]

There is virtually universal agreement among Christian historians on the fact that the institutionalization of the early church brought about the demise of charismatic gifts. Therefore, from a historical perspective, charisma did not cease as a result of any scriptural mandate or as the result of the closing of the biblical canon. Instead, the historical evidence suggests that the sociological emphasis on the monarchial bishop contributed to the decline of charisma.

23. Ackland, *Toward a Pentecostal Theology*, 412.
24. Ash, "Decline of Ecstatic Prophecy," 249.

THE DECLINE OF CHARISMATIC MANIFESTATIONS

Beginning with the fifth century, the writings that come down to us from Christian history show that charismatic workings became something that was limited to a select number of "spiritual elite." The medieval Christian church began to institutionalize a spiritual hierarchy (namely, bishops) that resulted in a total inverse of what the New Testament authors describe as normative. In addressing this monumental shift, Campenhausen writes:

> Paul neither knows of nor desiderates any official whose job it is to take charge of this testimony within the church, and to be its continuing representative. The edifying and formation of the church is left entirely to the Spirit, who does indeed follow from the apostolic witness and the Gospel, but who operates freely through the Body of Christ, and whose manifold gifts cannot be organized in any kind of official system.[25]

As a result of this monumental shift within the church, it is evident that a monopolization of charisma took place. There was an inherent conflict between ecclesiastical institutionalization and spontaneous acts of prayer and worship. As such, it was common for episcopacy to develop at the expense of the exercising of spiritual gifts, especially that of speaking in tongues.[26] Not only did the institutionalization of the church result in a dramatic reduction of charismatic activity, but those who were in the position of spiritual authority began to write against the practice of spiritual gifts.

One influential person who played a significant role in the decline of charismatic gifts within the church was Augustine of Hippo (354–430 AD). As one of the most influential theological writers in church history, Augustine's contributions have had a lasting impact on the church. Within his numerous writings, Augustine speaks of speaking in tongues as having diminished and then ceased, stating:

> Likewise, this statement of mine is indeed true: "These miracles were not allowed to last until our times lest the soul ever seek visible thing and the human race grow cold because of familiarity with those things whose novelty enkindled it." For not even now, when a hand is laid on the baptized, do they receive the Holy Spirit in such a way that they speak with the tongues of all nations; nor are the sick now healed by the passing shadow of the preachers of

25. Campenhausen, *Ecclesiastical Authority*, 150.
26. Hunter, "Tongues-Speech," 137.

Christ. Even though such things happened at that time, manifestly
these ceased later.[27]

For Augustine, the practice of speaking in tongues had diminished to the
point that there should be no expectations for its use within the church.
The reason for this view stems from his misunderstanding of the purpose
of speaking in tongues.

From his writings, it appears that Augustine viewed the gift of tongues
as the ability to speak in unlearned human languages to spread the gospel. By now, the gift of tongues had been incorporated into the corporate
church as it spread the gospel to all languages. Augustine writes:

> For at that time the church was not yet spread out through the
> circle of lands, that the organs of Christ were speaking in all the
> nations. Then it was filled-up into one, with respect to which it
> was being proclaimed in every one of them. Now the entire body
> of Christ is speaking in all the languages. To those which it is not
> yet speaking, it will be speaking in the future. For the church will
> multiply until it shall seize all the languages [in the entire world].
> Hold fast with us until that time had come near, and you shall ar-
> rive with us to that which had not yet drawn near. I intend to teach
> you to speak in all the languages. I am in the body of Christ, I am
> in the church of Christ. If the body of Christ is now speaking in all
> the languages, [then] also I am indeed speaking in all languages; to
> me it is that of Greek, Syrian, Hebrew, it is of every nation, because
> in unity, I am of every nation.[28]

From this misunderstanding of speaking in tongues, Augustine viewed the
sign of speaking in tongues in association with Spirit reception as limited
to the early church.

This mistaken view of speaking in tongues further led Augustine to
propose that the sign of Spirit reception had become love. In an exposition
of 1 John 3:23, Augustine declares:

> In the first days the Holy Spirit fell upon the believers, and they
> spoke in tongues that they hadn't learned, as the Spirit gave them
> to speak. These signs were appropriate for the time. For it was nec-
> essary that the Holy Spirit be signified thus in all tongues, because
> the gospel of God was going to traverse all tongues throughout the
> earth. That was the sign that was given, and it passed. Is it expected

27. Augustine, *Retractations*, 55.
28. Augustine, *Expositions of the Psalms*, 489.

now of those upon whom a hand is imposed, so that they may receive the Holy Spirit, that they speak in tongues?[29]

Augustine conflates the work of the Spirit at Pentecost (as evidenced by speaking in tongues) with the work of the Spirit in spreading the gospel throughout the world in love. These are clearly two separate works of the Spirit and should not be seen as identical in their purpose or function.

Beginning with Augustine's writings, there is a clear shift in the theological acceptance of speaking in tongues. The historical evidence is clear that within the medieval period, a stark divide from the patristic era occured. While the patristic fathers accepted the charismatic gifts as the normative workings of the Spirit within the church, the medieval institutionalization of the church moved to marginalizing these gifts. With the rise of Pope Leo the Great (400–61 AD) and his perspective that there was no value in "spectacular" charisma, the practice of charismatic gifts within the church was given a severe blow that it would not soon recover from.[30]

However, to say that charisma (and specifically, speaking in tongues) went away entirely during this period would not be accurate. In explaining the complicated relationship with speaking in tongues that was generated during this period, Burgess writes:

> The medieval Roman Church developed a dual standard in the treatment of tongue-speaking. While condemning the ability to speak in an unknown language and interpreting the utterance as an evidence of demon possession, the church also honored a few of its more illustrious number for their tongues-speaking . . . including the phenomenon . . . on their behalf in the canonization process.[31]

Therefore, it is evident that the charismatic manifestations designed to be available to every believer had become institutionalized and relegated to only the spiritual elite. The church's institutionalization of charisma was precisely the opposite of how Paul envisioned charisma operating within the Corinthian church (1 Cor 12–14). The regulating of charismatic activity to only the "spiritual elite" resulted in a dramatic shift of power to the clerical aristocracy and had a devastating impact on the church. To this point, Campenhausen argues that this period resulted in an environment where

29. Augustine, *Homilies*, 97.

30. Hunter, "Tongues-Speech," 135.

31. Burgess, "Medieval Examples," 25.

"free charismatic gifts which might set themselves up in rivalry to office are now almost unknown."[32] It is no surprise, then, that a Pentecostal perspective on charismatic gifts, drawing from the events of Pentecost, envisions that charisma should be available to all believers (Acts 2:16–18).

While the historical record reveals that charisma declined after the patristic period due to the institutionalization of the church, it would not be accurate to say that these manifestations ceased completely. Throughout the medieval church, there remained a handful of people who supported and practiced spiritual manifestations, such as Hildegard of Bingen (1098–1179), Francis of Assisi (1181–1226), Thomas Aquinas (1225–74), Vincent Ferrier (1350–1419), and Ignatius of Loyola (1491–1556).[33] Once the ecclesiastical dust had settled from the Reformation, the church began to move into a period of newfound freedom from the institutional powers which would quench spiritual manifestations. As a result, revivals marked by spiritual manifestations started to become more and more commonplace within the church. A few examples include George Fox (1624–91) and the Quakers, John Wesley (1703–91), and Edward Irving (1792–1834). The historical record reveals that slowly but steadily, the Holy Spirit was leading the church to an awakening to the purpose and power of spiritual manifestations.

SPEAKING IN TONGUES AND THE HISTORICAL DEVELOPMENT OF DOCTRINE

In examining the historical analysis of doctrines surrounding speaking in tongues, it is essential first to understand how doctrine was developed throughout church history and why it formed the way it did. The central focus of Christian doctrine is the pursuit of understanding God's self-revelation through his word. The special revelatory acts of God in both the person of Christ and the inspiration of Holy Sripture requires that any serious Christian spend considerable time pondering these divine actions. Therefore, understanding the development of Christian doctrine is essential for both its historical significance and its practical theological implications. Furthermore, understanding the general nature of doctrinal

32. Campenhausen, *Ecclesiastical Authority*, 265.

33. For more information on spiritual manifestations in the medieval period, see Burgess, *Christian Peoples*.

development will aid in the task of establishing a doctrinal foundation for speaking in tongues.

The central concern of doctrinal accuracy is not merely possessing true beliefs but inspiring correct behavior. To separate either confession or conduct from one's understanding of biblical doctrine creates an unbiblical view of that subject. Therefore, the development of Christian doctrine is not intended to merely create a philosophical framework of belief (although it should include this). Instead, doctrine is also designed to have a transformational impact on a person's actions. The necessity of doctrine possessing both orthodoxy (correct belief) and orthopraxy (correct behavior) is supported by the apostle James's statement regarding demonic beings (Jas 2:19). The fact that even demons hold correct beliefs about God emphasizes the need for Christian doctrine to go beyond mental assent to include a way of living. It is precisely to this failure to live out the Christian faith that Paul attributes the reason for the "doctrine of devils" (1 Tim 4:1). Without the foundation of doctrine (orthodoxy and orthopraxy), Christianity has no gospel. Just as faith without works is incomplete (Jas 2:26), doctrine consisting of only belief and devoid of behavior is wholly insufficient.

Therefore, the historical development and defense of biblical doctrine has done more than protect a belief system—it has guarded a way of living (2 Cor 5:17; Jas 1:22–27). It is through the wisdom accrued throughout church history that historical doctrines can empower Christians today in their efforts to faithfully live and obey Christ's commands (Matt 28:20). So vital is the role of historical theology to the church that there is little doubt that the church could not stand as an organization without its influence. It is an often-repeated refrain—but the truth remains—that we stand on the shoulders of those who preceded us as saints and scholars of our sacred text. As Protestants, we are wise to study the contributions of those throughout church history and to recognize our indebtedness to them.

Yet, if the history of doctrinal development throughout the ages has revealed anything, it has proven that the task of producing doctrinal truths is a lengthy and challenging process. There are three essential reasons why doctrine developed the way it did: Firstly, the Bible was not designed as a systematic theology textbook. Instead, it is a collection of narratives, songs, poems, letters, and apocalyptic writings. Because of this, the task of developing doctrine requires time and a careful examination of the whole canon of Scripture to ensure that false doctrines do not evolve in the process. While the early church did not set forth a "systematic theology," its apologetic defense of the Christian faith against early critics can be clearly seen (1 Pet 3:15; 2 Cor 10:5; 2 Tim 4:1–5). When the apostles confessed their beliefs regarding the life, death, and resurrection of Christ, they did so in the face of vicious attacks from both the secular and the religious communities. Furthermore, while Christianity was still in its infancy, the early church was forced to deal with attacks from within the Christian movement itself (Gal 1:7; 2 Pet 2:1–3; 1 John 4:1). It is from the apologetic foundation laid down by the apostles—as they sought to defend the gospel of Christ—that the development of doctrinal creeds began to arise throughout the patristic age.

Secondly, the Bible is a collection of books. This means that the one book contains various authors with diverse geographical, cultural, and historical perspectives from which they write. This diversity within unity found within Scripture mirrors the diversity within unity seen within the triune nature of God (Matt 3:16; John 14:26; Acts 10:38; 2 Cor 13:14). And while the Bible's diversity within unity is beautiful, it also requires that doctrinal themes be traced throughout these inspired writings. Such a task necessitates the passage of time and the careful discipline of many theologians to properly lay out scriptural truths. As defenders of sacred truths, theologians throughout church history have sought to refute heresies that would divide Scripture's unifying message. Doctrines develop from an interactive process between the inspired Scripture and the various communities that have interpreted Scripture throughout history. Thus, while doctrines develop out of the Bible, they do so within a human community of disciples who approach Scripture within their cultural framework.

Thirdly, the development of doctrine involves a human process that the church carries out. This is not to say that this development does not have a divine origin or influence—for the church is being built by Jesus Christ (Matt 16:13–20). While the Bible is perfectly clear that its source is God breathed (2 Tim 3:16), God has chosen to facilitate the formation of Scripture through human agents. These human agents did not write according to their will but instead, through the Spirit, wrote from divine inspiration (2 Pet 1:21). While orthodoxy states that the divine-human interworking that created Holy Scripture is free from error, it would not be correct to say that every "scripturally" based doctrine is true. That is to say, not every doctrine developed throughout church history which used Scripture as its pretext for being accurate should be considered to be orthodox. Therefore, the task of developing Christian doctrine requires a posture of humility as each generation of the church receives and advances the task of rightly divining the word of truth (2 Tim 2:15). Therefore, the responsibility of developing doctrine—while indeed guided by the Spirit—necessitates the continual commitment of human agents.

A common argument against the formation of doctrine on speaking in tongues focuses on the relatively small number of scriptural texts that address the subject. There are thirty-five references to glossolalia in Scripture. Twenty-eight of those are found in 1 Corinthians, and the majority of the rest appear in the Acts of the Apostles. From this "limited" number of references to the phenomenon of speaking in tongues, some argue that an authoritative doctrine on the subject cannot be properly formed. But if the brevity of a theological truth were the determining factor for deciding its authority, there would be more than a few cardinal doctrines which would lose their standing. For example, more is said about speaking in tongues in Scripture than about the virgin birth of Christ, the ordinance of Holy Communion, the ordination of women, and many eschatological doctrines. Therefore, the "limited" biblical support for speaking in tongues fails to stand as a valid argument for dismissing the formation of a theological doctrine of the phenomenon. In fact, the simple reality that speaking in tongues is found as a reoccurring phenomenon associated with the moving of the Spirit necessitates the formation of doctrinal explanation for its appearance.

This is an essential fact when it comes to doctrines surrounding speaking in tongues. Many cessationists have argued against the validity of the phenomenon primarily based on its relative doctrinal "newness." While this chapter will argue that the practice of glossolalia is not new, the fact of the matter remains—the timing of a doctrine's formation is irrelevant to its scriptural accuracy. Furthermore, there are a plethora of historical examples of attacks against a doctrine based upon its "newness" that proved to be in error. Just one example of this can be found in Martin Luther's reformational doctrine of *sola fide*. The sixteenth-century discovery (or perhaps better put, rediscovery) of the doctrine of justification by faith alone by Martin Luther was vigorously rejected by the church of that day for the ways this "new" ideology reshaped biblical, theological, and sociological norms.[34] However, rather than *sola fide* being a "new" doctrine, it was a renewing doctrine that sought the restoration of biblical truth established

---

34. For an account of the transformative nature of Martin Luther's theology, see Metaxas, *Martin Luther*.

within Scripture. Likewise, the twentieth-century discovery (again, better put, rediscovery) of charismatic doctrine does not seek to create a "new" doctrine but rather the restoration of biblical truths found within Scripture.

Just as God's self-revelation through Scripture was not an instantaneous act, the development of doctrine should not be expected to be static. In Jaroslav Pelikan's five-volume masterpiece, *The Christian Tradition: A History of the Development of Doctrine*, the author underscores this point by stating:

> The relation between believing, teaching, and confessing also implies that both the subject matter and the source material for the history of the development of doctrine will shift, gradually but steadily, as we trace it through the history of the church.[35]

Given this fact—while the canon of Scripture may be closed—the development of doctrine will continue to be a necessary task throughout the entirety of the church age. As each succeeding generation continues to face heretical attacks on doctrine—either attacks on truths of orthodoxy or of orthopraxy—there is a constant need for the church to defend "sound doctrine" (1 Tim 1:10; 2 Tim 4:3; Titus 2:1). Therefore, at the core of doctrinal development is the issue of preserving the current church and facilitating the health of the future church.

While an analysis of historical doctrine can serve as a defense against the church falling for "novel" doctrines (1 Tim 6:3), the accuracy of any particular doctrine should not be judged based solely upon its relative "newness." Just as there are heretical doctrines in modern times, even the early church had to deal with doctrinal fallacies (Titus 1:9; Heb 11:13; Rom 16:17). Therefore, it is clear that the accuracy of a doctrine should not be dependent upon the historical timing of its development but rather on the truthfulness of its claims based upon Scripture. As such, the classical Pentecostal position of Spirit baptism as evidenced by speaking in other tongues need not be abandoned merely due to its relative "newness" as a doctrinal position. Instead, tongues as an initial physical evidence of Spirit baptism must stand or fall only on its biblical merits.

---

35. Pelikan, *Catholic Tradition*, 48.

CONCLUSION

When it comes to spiritual manifestations, the biblical burden of proof rests upon the cessationist to show from Scripture where the cessation of charisma is supported. Since the practice of charismatic manifestations is clearly taught to be the normative pattern of the early church and there is historical evidence that this practice continued throughout the church age, then the Pentecostal position on spiritual manifestations should be fully embraced by the church today.

While the doctrine of initial physical evidence is relatively "new" from a historical perspective, this fact alone should not disqualify it. Nor should the classical Pentecostal position of evidential tongues be accepted based on its prominence in the last century of Pentecostalism. Instead, the only proof that Pentecostals must point to, whether for or against the doctrinal position of initial physical evidence, must be its scriptural foundation. While being informed of the historical aspects of speaking in tongues, those who find the Lukan description of Spirit baptism to be sufficient evidence for the doctrine of initial physical evidence should continue to stand on that belief.

6

A Multidisciplinary Perspective of Speaking in Tongues

INTRODUCTION

Pentecostals have long claimed that Spirit baptism is an essential part of the "full" gospel. This understanding that the work of the Spirit to baptize believers as a subsequent work to salvation is central to a holistic approach to Pentecostal pneumatology. Yet, this Pentecostal holistic, or "full," gospel cannot adequately influence our world unless it interacts within a full (multidisciplinary) approach. Yong points out that "our claim to embody a robustly holistic spirituality will be hollow unless purged through the critical fire of an equally robust multi-disciplinary analysis."[1] Since the Pentecostal perspective of Spirit activity in this world claims that it touches every part of this world, then it is impossible to isolate the presence and activity of the Spirit to the biblical/theological arena. As a sign of Spirit baptism, speaking in tongues should be able to stand against the scrutiny of a multidisciplinary investigation into its validity.

By definition, speaking in tongues is unintelligible language; however, the Pentecostal should not assume that its practice has nothing to "say" within a multidisciplinary perspective. In fact, the Pentecostal should work to "interpret" our distinctive practice of speaking in tongues through the lens of various disciplines to reveal ways in which this Spirit-inspired speech can "speak" to our present day. Pentecostal spirituality offers a

1. Yong, "Academic Glossolalia?," 79.

unique way of viewing the world, for it presupposes that this life must be lived in and through the Spirit. As such, Pentecostal pneumatology should stir our imagination to envision new ways in which speaking in tongues can "speak" to the religion-and-science discussion.

The first step in equipping Pentecostals to engage in dialogue from a multidisciplinary perspective seems to be that Pentecostals themselves first understand the practice of speaking in tongues. Only by understanding their unique Pentecostal "voice" can Pentecostals begin to confidently explain and defend the practice of speaking in tongues to the non-Pentecostal community. A mistaken assumption would be to suppose that Pentecostal adherents understand their experience with speaking in tongues. There can be no denying the Pentecostal emphasis on experiential knowledge and the importance Pentecostals place on having such Spirit encounters. Yet, the fact remains that Pentecostals' experiential knowledge fails to be convincing evidence for the one who has never experienced the phenomenon of speaking in tongues. Thus, it is vitally important that Pentecostal adherents go beyond the experiential knowledge of speaking in tongues and add to their experience supporting evidence that can defend the substance of their experience. Without such supporting evidence, the Pentecostal's experience can easily be discredited by those who do not understand the purpose of speaking in tongues.

Furthermore, I would submit that supporting evidence is helpful even for those who practice speaking in tongues. Given the nature of the phenomenon of speaking in tongues, Pentecostal adherents should be equipped with a rational defense from across various academic disciplines as to the validity of their practice. This approach would empower Pentecostal adherents on two fronts. First, a multidisciplinary understanding of speaking in tongues would bolster a deeper appreciation for the purpose and power of speaking in tongues. A Pentecostal spirituality that views the experience of speaking in tongues within a broader multidisciplinary perspective will undoubtedly reveal new ways in which speaking in tongues can communicate "the wonderful works of God" (Acts 2:11). Secondly, a multidisciplinary understanding of speaking in tongues will empower Pentecostal practitioners to be able to defend their distinctive belief and practice better. Through a greater understanding of the ways in which speaking in tongues "speaks" across various disciplines, the Pentecostal can better defend this Spirit-inspired phenomenon.

A CASE STUDY: AN APOLOGETIC OF GLOSSOLALIA WORKSHOP

The following provides a look at empirical research conducted by the author to discover Pentecostal adherents' knowledge of and attitudes toward speaking in tongues. Until this point, no research existed that examined the efficacy of educating Pentecostal adherents in the doctrine, practice, or apologetic defense of speaking in tongues. This lacuna in the research inspired the author to discover the efficacy of a workshop designed to train self-identified Pentecostals in the doctrine, practice, and apologetic defense of speaking in tongues. In order to accomplish this, the author created the *Apologetic of Glossolalia Workshop*, which taught participants about speaking in tongues from a multidisciplinary perspective.

The workshop was a six-hour-long event with eighty-two participants who all self-identified as Pentecostals. The methodology of examining the workshop's efficacy required evaluating pre- and post-workshop questionnaires designed to detect changes in participants' knowledge of, attitudes toward, and behavior regarding speaking in tongues. The data-collection procedures for assessing participants' glossolalic knowledge and attitudes involved distributing questionnaires pre- and postworkshop. Behavioral changes in participants were evaluated through semi-structured interviews conducted six weeks postworkshop.

Analysis of the Case Study

Pentecostal Adherents Knowledge Assessment

According to the data collected using the pre- and postworkshop Knowledge Assessment Questionnaire,[2] only 44.4 percent of the participants agreed or strongly agreed that they had been adequately taught about speaking in tongues as a part of their Pentecostal experience prior to the workshop. However, after the workshop, 97.1 percent of participants agreed or strongly agreed that they had now been adequately taught about speaking in tongues. This data reveals a 52.7 percent jump in participants agreeing that they had experienced adequate teaching about the subject of speaking in tongues. The fact that a majority of the self-identified Pentecostal participants did not feel like they had ever been adequately taught about

2. See appendix 1.

speaking in tongues should be of concern for Pentecostals. However, the workshop proved significant in addressing these Pentecostal adherents' not being adequately trained about speaking in tongues.

Furthermore, the pre-workshop data disclosed that 52.8 percent of participants stated they did not feel confident explaining speaking in tongues to non-Pentecostals. However, the postworkshop data revealed that only 2.9 percent still felt they were not confident in explaining speaking in tongues to non-Pentecostals. This data shows a tremendous rise in confidence from the participants in their ability to accurately describe and defend their belief in speaking in tongues to non-Pentecostals. Furthermore, the marked increase in participants' confidence in defending speaking in tongues against non-Pentecostal inquiries provides further evidence that, if adequately trained, self-identified Pentecostals are willing to defend their practice of speaking in tongues.

Finally, the pre-workshop data revealed that only 16.7 percent of participants strongly agreed that they understood the proper function of speaking in tongues within the church. The postworkshop numbers provided a stark contrast, as 77.1 percent of participants strongly agreed that they now understood the proper function of speaking in tongues within the church after attending the workshop.

The significantly low percentage of Pentecostal adherents who know the biblically appropriate way speaking in tongues should operate within the church must be addressed within Pentecostalism. If Pentecostal adherents are not educated on the proper function of speaking in tongues within the church, there is a real danger that this spiritual manifestation will cease within Pentecostalism.

The data collected through the Knowledge Assessment Questionnaire emphasizes a significant increase in participants' knowledge about speaking in tongues as a result of the *Apologetic of Glossolalia Workshop*. Through a multidisciplinary approach to defending speaking in tongues, Pentecostal adherents experienced a notable rise in their knowledge of the subject.

Pentecostal Adherents Attitude Assessment

According to the data collected using the pre- and postworkshop Attitude Assessment Questionnaire,[3] 27.7 percent of the self-identified Pentecostal participants reported at the beginning of the workshop that they sometimes

3. See appendix 2.

wondered whether speaking in tongues was essential. However, the post-workshop data showed a dramatic decrease in this number. By the end of the workshop, only 8.4 percent of the participants still wondered if speaking in tongues was essential.

The fact that a meaningful percentage of Pentecostal adherents have doubts about the validity of speaking in tongues should be a significant area of concern for Pentecostalism. Additionally, it should highlight the need for systematic training in this area so that Pentecostal adherents can be confident in their distinguishing practice of speaking in tongues. The statistical contrast between the pre-workshop and postworkshop numbers indicates that a majority of the participants who came into the workshop with an attitude of uncertainty about speaking in tongues left the workshop feeling much more confident about its importance in their lives. The dramatic increase in participants' belief in the essentiality of speaking in tongues as a result of the *Apologetic of Glossolalia Workshop* is statistically significant and provides overwhelming evidence that Pentecostal adherents can be equipped to defend their distinctive practice of speaking in tongues. It is evident that educating Pentecostal adherents about speaking in tongues directly impacts their feelings on the subject. Therefore, it is essential to empower self-identified Pentecostals with a logical defense of speaking in tongues from a multidisciplinary perspective. Additionally, it should highlight the need for systematic training in this area so that Pentecostal adherents can be confident in their distinguishing practice of speaking in tongues.

Additionally, the Attitude Assessment Questionnaire data identified that 71.5 percent of participants expressed concern that speaking tongues is becoming less significant to Pentecostals. This data suggests a prominent sense of worry among self-identified Pentecostals regarding the future of speaking in tongues within Pentecostalism. Such concern from self-identified Pentecostals indicates the need for a concentrated effort within Pentecostalism to systematically address the role of speaking in tongues within the future of Pentecostalism. The best days of Pentecostalism do not have to be in its history. When you consider that Pentecostals are given an opportunity to show how tongue speech can "speak" into numerous areas of life through a multidisciplinary approach, the future of Pentecostalism is exciting. But for that to take place, Pentecostals must know how to defend their unique practice of speaking in tongues and be trained to seek

Spirit-inspired vision that will look for how the phenomenon can "speak" to our world today.

Pentecostal Adherents' Glossolalic Behavior

In order to assess any behavioral changes related to the *Apologetic of Glossolalia Workshop*, the author conducted semi-structured interviews six weeks postworkshop[4] to collect qualitative data relating to speaking in tongues as reported by the workshop participants. The researcher discovered that none of the interviewed participants felt like they had been effectively taught about the subject of speaking in tongues before attending the workshop. For most participants, what they had learned about the topic came from bits and pieces of sermons, but nothing that systematically covered the subject. The multidisciplinary approach sparked a desire to learn more about speaking in tongues and its relationship to Spirit empowerment in this present world.

When asked if they had noticed any changes in their engagement with speaking in tongues since the workshop, participants expressed that they possessed newfound confidence in glossolalic speech. Many confessed that while they had previously practiced speaking in tongues, their lack of knowledge about the subject had hindered their confidence in this spiritual activity. However, since attending the workshop, their increased confidence resulted in a much deeper sense of enjoyment in its practice. Without question, the participants expressed a direct correlation between an increase in knowledge about the subject of speaking in tongues and their increased practice of the phenomenon. To this point, many stated that they were now practicing glossolalic speech with more regularity since the workshop. Overall, the participants affirmed that the workshop had facilitated an increased enjoyment of glossolalic speech in their day-to-day lives.

Finally, when asked about the defense of their belief and practice of speaking in tongues, all the participants stated they felt more confident answering questions about speaking in tongues after the workshop. Since the workshop helped answer many of their own questions about speaking in tongues, the participants felt better equipped to answer the questions of others. Having been shown how speaking in tongues can be logically defended from a multidisciplinary perspective, participants felt an increased boldness in talking about speaking in tongues with non-Pentecostals. For

4. See appendix 3.

certain, this newfound confidence in the phenomenon of speaking in tongues brought about significant changes in behavior for the participants of the *Apologetic of Glossolalia Workshop*.

Theological Reflections on the Case Study

The research findings from this case study reveal that a significant amount of self-identified Pentecostal have not been adequately trained in the doctrine or practice of speaking in tongues. This research constitutes a warning for the Pentecostal Church: it must renew its focus on systematically teaching its distinctive doctrinal practice of speaking in tongues. A real danger exists that the next generation of self-identified Pentecostal believers will be Pentecostal in name only, having grown up with an association with the denomination but never having participated in the Pentecostal experience of speaking in tongues.

Furthermore, the case study revealed that the absence of training on the subject of speaking in tongues has resulted in self-identified Pentecostals struggling with a lack of confidence in their ability to practice and defend their belief in speaking in tongues. This research suggests that many Pentecostals are not equipped to defend their belief that speaking in tongues is valid today when confronted with cessationist teaching. The inability of Pentecostal adherents to biblically defend their distinctive practice should concern both the Pentecostal academy and the Pentecostal Church.

Therefore, the Pentecostal Church must actively educate its members in the doctrine, practice, and defense of speaking in tongues. This would ensure that both current and future generations of Pentecostal Christians are adequately trained in the importance of Spirit baptism as evidenced by speaking in tongues. The data suggests that a majority of self-identified Pentecostals studied had not been adequately taught about speaking in tongues as part of their Pentecostal experience. The fact that the current generation of self-identified Pentecostals feels inadequately prepared to defend their distinctive practice of speaking in tongues should alarm Pentecostalism regarding the future state of the movement. What one generation fails to teach and defend, the next generation will undoubtedly ignore and deny.

With this understanding, the Pentecostal Church and academy should embrace a renewed call to teaching and defending its distinctive practice of speaking in tongues. No apology needs to be made for continuing to espouse the multifaceted benefits of practicing the Spirit-induced phenomenon of speaking in tongues. Whether from a biblical/theological, practical theology, social science, or historical perspective, speaking in tongues passes a multidisciplinary test as a valid and valued spiritual manifestation. Therefore, let the Pentecostal Church continue to preach, teach, and equip each generation of adherents not just to understand our distinctive practice of speaking in tongues but to be active participants in this Spirit-inspired power.

CONCLUSION

The underlying purpose behind this book and the *Apologetic of Glossolalia Workshop* is to equip self-identifying Pentecostals to adequately defend their distinctive practice of speaking in other tongues. Through a multidisciplinary defense of speaking in tongues, the Pentecostal is provided with a powerful resource in two ways.

First, through the multidisciplinary approach, the Pentecostal can combat a variety of attacks aimed at the practice of speaking in tongues. Since most of the focus of defending the veracity of tongue speech centers around its biblical/theological viability, understanding what the other disciplines have to say about the subject serves the Pentecostal well in their apologetic defense. This is especially true for the Pentecostal adherent who seeks to defend the practice of speaking in tongues to nonbelievers. The apostle Paul warned the Corinthian church about speaking in tongues leading to nonbelievers assuming they were crazy (1 Cor 14:23). This warning also applies to the modern church and the way in which it presents the phenomenon of speaking in tongues. However, through a multidisciplinary understanding of speaking in other tongues, Pentecostals are able to rationally defend their practice and bring logical credibility to their claims concerning its power.

Secondly, a multidisciplinary approach to speaking in tongues allows Pentecostals to appreciate this Spirit-inspired practice more deeply. Through the lens of a multidisciplinary approach, the Pentecostal can see more clearly the wonders afforded them through the phenomenon of speaking in tongues. This deeper perspective cannot help but enrich the practice for Pentecostals and empower them to continue to practice Spirit-inspired tongue speech as a means of prayer and praise to God.

As Pentecostalism continues to grow throughout the twenty-first century, it is essential that Pentecostals intentionally think through how they will educate adherents on their distinctive practice of speaking in tongues. Failure to adequately train Pentecostals on the purpose and practice of speaking in tongues will undoubtedly lead to the Pentecostal Church's minimizing its value. Therefore, the systematic defense of speaking in tongues does more than protect a doctrinal belief—it ensures the continuation of Pentecostalism's distinguishing means of Spirit-directed communication with God. As such, the phenomenon of speaking in tongues is a distinct Pentecostal practice worth promoting in this generation and preserving for future generations.

Appendix 1

Knowledge-Assessment Questionnaire

Instructions:
Please circle, on a scale of 1 to 5, your overall assessment of
your knowledge relative to the statements provided, with **1
indicating strong disagreement, 2 indicating disagreement, 3
indicating neutral, 4 indicating agreement,** and **5 indicating
strong agreement**.

Assessment Factor	Strongly Disagree	Disagree	Neutral	Agree	Strongly Agree
1. I was taught adequately about speaking in tongues as part of my Pentecostal experience.	1	2	3	4	5
2. I am confident in explaining glossolalia to non-Pentecostals	1	2	3	4	5
3. I know what cessationists believe concerning speaking in tongues.	1	2	3	4	5
4. The apostle Paul taught that speaking in tongues was greater than prophecy.	1	2	3	4	5
5. Speaking in tongues is an aid in missional empowerment.	1	2	3	4	5
6. I understand the doctrine of initial physical evidence.	1	2	3	4	5

Assessment Factor	Strongly Disagree	Disagree	Neutral	Agree	Strongly Agree
7. I have previously been taught about how speaking in tongues integrates with the social sciences.	1	2	3	4	5
8. Speaking in tongues is fundamentally prayer and praise to God.	1	2	3	4	5
9. The interpretation of tongues is the equivalent of prophecy.	1	2	3	4	5
10. I understand the proper function of speaking in tongues within the church.	1	2	3	4	5

Appendix 2

Attitude-Assessment Questionnaire

Instructions:
Please circle, on a scale of 1 to 5, your overall attitude regarding the statements provided, with **1 indicating strong disagreement, 2 indicating disagreement, 3 indicating neutral, 4 indicating agreement, and 5 indicating strong agreement.**

Assessment Factor	Strongly Disagree	Disagree	Neutral	Agree	Strongly Agree
1. I feel comfortable talking about glossolalia to others.	1	2	3	4	5
2. Speaking in tongues is a source of joy for me.	1	2	3	4	5
3. I sometimes feel guilty that I do not speak in tongues more.	1	2	3	4	5
4. I sometimes wonder if speaking in tongues is really important.	1	2	3	4	5
5. I feel uncertain about the impact of speaking in tongues in my life.	1	2	3	4	5
6. I am comfortable with singing in tongues.	1	2	3	4	5
7. I feel the Holy Spirit working in me when I speak in tongues.	1	2	3	4	5
8. I am active in my practice of speaking in other tongues.	1	2	3	4	5

Assessment Factor	Strongly Disagree	Disagree	Neutral	Agree	Strongly Agree
9. I sometimes feel unworthy to speak in tongues.	1	2	3	4	5
10. I am concerned that speaking in tongues is becoming less significant to Pentecostals.	1	2	3	4	5

Appendix 3

Semi-structured Interview

Instructions:
Please answer each of the following questions to the best of your ability.

INTERVIEW QUESTIONS

1. How many years have you been a Pentecostal?

2. How many years have you practiced speaking in tongues?

3. Had you been taught much about speaking in tongues before the workshop? Explain.

4. How has your attitude toward speaking in tongues changed, if at all, since the workshop? Explain.

5. Has the Holy Spirit used speaking in tongues to work in your life since the workshop? Explain.

6. Have you noticed any changes in your engagement with speaking in tongues since the workshop? Explain.

7. Do you believe that what your learned about speaking in other tongues has positively influenced your practice of speaking in other tongues? Explain.

8. Do you believe you will speak in tongues more often in the future because of the workshop? Explain.

9. Do you feel better equipped to defend your belief and practice of speaking in tongues since the workshop? Explain.

10. Would you recommend that other Pentecostals learn more about speaking in tongues? Why or why not?

Bibliography

Ackland, Randal H. *Toward a Pentecostal Theology of Glossolalia.* Cleveland: Centre for Pentecostal Theology, 2020.

Allison, Gregg. *Historical Theology: An Introduction to Christian Doctrine.* Grand Rapids: Zondervan Academic, 2011.

Althouse, Peter. *Spirit of the Last Days: Pentecostal Eschatology in Conversation with Jürgen Moltmann.* New York: T. & T. Clark International, 2003.

Anderson, Allan. *An Introduction to Pentecostalism: Global Charismatic Christianity.* Cambridge: Cambridge University Press, 2004.

Anderson, Ray S. *Ministry on the Fireline: A Practical Theology for an Empowered Church.* Pasadena, CA: Fuller Seminary, 1998.

———. *The Shape of Practical Theology: Empowering Ministry with Theological Praxis,* Downers Grove: InterVarsity, 2001.

Ash, James L., Jr. "The Decline of Ecstatic Prophecy in the Early Church." *Theological Studies* 37.2 (1976) 227–52.

Augustine. *Expositions on the Psalms.* Vol. 6. The Works of Saint Augustine: A Translation for the 21st Century. New York: New City Press, 2005.

———. *Homilies on the First Epistle of John.* Vol. 3, no. 14. The Works of Saint Augustine: A Translation for the 21st Century. Translated by Boniface Ramsey. Edited by Daniel E. Doyle and Thomas Martin. Hyde Park, NY: New City, 2008.

———. *The Retractations.* Fathers of the Church Patristic Series 60. Translated by Mary Inez Bogan. Washington, DC: The Catholic University of America Press, 1999.

Austin, John. *How to Do Things with Words.* Oxford: Oxford University Press, 1975.

Ballard, Paul, and John Pritchard. *Practical Theology in Action: Christian Thinking in the Service of Church and Society.* London: Society for Promoting Christian Knowledge, 1996.

Bartholomew, Craig G., et al., eds. *After Pentecost: Language and Biblical Interpretation.* Vol. 2. Grand Rapids: Zondervan, 2001.

Beare, Frank W. "Speaking with Tongues: A Critical Survey of the New Testament Evidence." *Journal of Biblical Literature* 83.3 (1964) 229–46.

Brannan, Rick. *The Apostolic Fathers: A New Translation.* Bellingham, WA: Lexham, 2017.

"Brief History of the Assemblies of God." Apostolic Archives International Inc. https://www.apostolicarchives.com/articles/article/8801925/173629.htm.

Bromiley, Geoffrey W., ed. *The International Standard Bible Encyclopedia.* Grand Rapids: Eerdmans, 1979.

BIBLIOGRAPHY

Bruce, F. F. *The Book of Acts*. Rev. ed. The New International Commentary on the New Testament. Grand Rapids: Eerdmans, 1988.

Brumback, Carl. *Tongues: Rescinded or Rejected?* Siloam Springs, AR: Offspring, 2013.

Burgess, Stanley M., ed. *Christian Peoples of the Spirit: A Documentary History of Pentecostal Spirituality from the Early Church to the Present*. New York: New York University Press, 2011.

———. "Medieval Examples of Charismatic Piety in the Roman Catholic Church." In *Perspectives on the New Pentecostalism*, edited by Russell P. Spittler, 14–26. Grand Rapids: Baker Book House, 1976.

Campenhausen, Hans von. *Ecclesiastical Authority and Spiritual Power in the Church of the First Three Centuries*. Peabody, MA: Hendrickson, 1997.

Carson, D. A. *Showing the Spirit: A Theological Exposition of 1 Corinthians 12–14*. Grand Rapids: Baker, 1987.

Cartledge, Mark. *Charismatic Glossolalia: An Empirical-Theological Study*. Aldershot: Ashgate, 2002.

———. *The Mediation of the Spirit: Interventions in Practical Theology*. Grand Rapids: Eerdmans, 2015.

Cho, Youngmo. "Spirit and Kingdom in Luke-Acts: Proclamation as the Primary Role of the Spirit in Relation to the Kingdom of God in Luke-Acts." *Asian Journal of Pentecostal Studies* 6.2 (2003) 173–97.

———. *Spirit and Kingdom in the Writings of Luke and Paul: An Attempt to Reconcile These Concepts*. Milton Keynes, UK: Paternoster, 2005.

Coulson, Jesse E., and Ray W. Johnson. "Glossolalia and Internal-External Locus of Control." *Journal of Psychology and Theology* 5.4 (1977) 312–17.

Cross, Terry. "The Divine-Human Encounter Towards a Pentecostal Theology of Experience." *Pneuma* 31.1 (2009) 3–34.

Cutten, George Barton. *Speaking with Tongues: Historically and Psychologically Considered*. Vol. 9. Yale University Press, 1927.

Dempster, Murray W. "The Church's Moral Witness: A Study of Glossolalia in Luke's Theology of Acts." *Paraclete* 23.1 (1989) 1–7.

Dorries, David W. "Edward Irving and the 'Standing Sign' of Spirit Baptism." In *Initial Evidence: Historical and Biblical Perspectives on the Pentecostal Doctrine of Spirit Baptism*, edited by Gary McGee, 41–56. Eugene, OR: Wipf & Stock, 1991.

Dunn, James D. G. *Baptism in the Holy Spirit*. Philadelphia: Westminister, 1970.

———. *Jesus and the Spirit: A Study of the Religious and Charismatic Experience of Jesus and the First Christians as Reflected in the New Testament*. Grand Rapids: Eerdmans, 1997.

Ellison, Christopher G. "Religious Involvement and Subjective Well-Being." *Journal of Health and Social Behavior* 32.1 (1991) 80–99.

Ervin, Howard M. *Spirit Baptism: A Biblical Investigation*. Peabody, MA: Hendrickson, 1987.

Evans, Rand B. "William James, 'The Principles of Psychology,' and Experimental Psychology." *The American Journal of Psychology* 103.4 (1990) 433–47.

Fee, Gordon D. *God's Empowering Presence: The Holy Spirit in the Letters of Paul*. Peabody, MA: Hendrickson, 1995.

———. *Paul, the Spirit, and the People of God*. Peabody, MA: Hendrickson, 1996.

———. *The First Epistle to the Corinthians*. The New International Commentary on the New Testament. Grand Rapids: Eerdmans, 2014.

Furnish, Victor. *New Testament Theology: The Theology of the First Letter to the Corinthians*. New York: Cambridge University Press, 1999.

Glasser, Arthur F. *Announcing the Kingdom: The Story of God's Mission in the Bible*. Grand Rapids: Baker Academic, 2003.

Goodman, Felicitas D. *Speaking in Tongues: A Cross-Cultural Study of Glossolalia*. Eugene, OR: Wipf & Stock, 2008.

Hamar, Paul. *The Book of First Corinthians*. Springfield, MO: Gospel, 1980.

Hilary of Poitiers. *On the Trinity*. Nicene and Post-Nicene Fathers. Peabody, MA: Henderickson, 1999.

Hine, Virginia H. "Pentecostal Glossolalia toward a Functional Interpretation." *Journal for the Scientific Study of Religion* 8.2 (1969) 211–26.

Holdcraft, L. Thomas. *The Holy Spirit: A Pentecostal Interpretation*. Abbotsford, BC: CeeTeC, 1999.

Hollenweger, Walter J. *Pentecostalism: Origins and Developments Worldwide*. Peabody, MA: Hendrickson, 1997.

Horton, Stanley M. *The Book of Acts*. Springfield: Gospel, 1981.

———. *What the Bible Says about the Holy Spirit*. Springfield, MO: Gospel, 2007.

———. *I & II Corinthians: A Logion Press Commentary*. Springfield, MO: Logion, 2012.

Hunter, Harold D. "Tongues-Speech: A Patristic Analysis." *Journal of the Evangelical Theological Society* 23.2 (1980) 125–37.

Irenaeus. *Against Heresies*. Edited by Alexander Roberts and James Donaldson. Self-published, CreateSpace, 2012.

Jacobsen, Douglas. *A Reader in Pentecostal Theology: Voices from the First Generation*. Bloomington, IN: Indiana University Press, 2006.

———. *Thinking in the Spirit: Theologies of the Early Pentecostal Movement*. Bloomington: Indiana University Press, 2003.

Jefford, Clayton N. *The Apostolic Fathers: An Essential Guide*. Nashville: Abingdon, 2005.

Jividen, Jimmy. *Glossolalia: From God or Man?* Fort Worth, TX: Star Bible, 1971.

Johnson, Alan F. *1 Corinthians*. The IVP New Testament Commentary Series. Downers Grove, IL: InterVarsity, 2004.

Johnson, Van. "Fulfillment of God's Promise in the Soon-to-Return King." In *Pentecostals in the 21st Century: Identity, Beliefs, Praxis*, edited by Corneliu Constantineanu and Christopher J. Scobie, 181–201. Eugene, OR: Cascade, 2018.

Kärkkäinen, Veli-Matti. *An Introduction to Ecclesiology: Ecumenical, Historical, and Global Perspectives*. Downers Grove, IL: InterVarsity, 2002.

———. *Pneumatology: The Holy Spirit in Ecumenical, International, and Contextual Perspective*. Grand Rapids: Baker Academic, 2018.

Kay, William K. "The Mind, Behavior, and Glossolalia—A Psychological Perspective." In *Speaking in Tongues: Multi-Disciplinary Perspectives*, edited by Mark J. Cartledge, 174–205. Waynesboro, GA: Paternoster, 2006.

Keener, Craig. *Acts: An Exegetical Commentary*. Grand Rapids: Baker Academic, 2013.

———. *Gift and Giver: The Holy Spirit for Today*. Grand Rapids: Baker Academic, 2020.

———. *Spirit Hermeneutics: Reading Scripture in Light of Pentecost*. Grand Rapids: Eerdmans, 2016.

———. "Why Does Luke Use Tongues as a Sign of the Spirit's Empowerment?" *Journal of Pentecostal Theology* 15.2 (2007) 177–84.

Kéri, Szabolcs, et al. "Enhanced Verbal Statistical Learning in Glossolalia." *Cognitive Science* 44.7 (2020).

Kildhal, John P. *The Psychology of Speaking in Tongues.* New York: Harper & Row, 1972.

Kydd, Ronald. *Charismatic Gifts in the Early Church: The Gifts of the Spirit in the First 300 Years.* Peabody, MA: Hendrickson, 2014.

Land, Steven Jack. *Pentecostal Spirituality: A Passion for the Kingdom.* London: Sheffield Academic Press, 1993.

Lim, David. *Spiritual Gifts: A Fresh Look.* Springfield, MO: Gospel, 1991.

Linzey, Verna M. *The Baptism with the Holy Spirit: The Reception of the Holy Spirit as Confirmed by Speaking in Tongues.* Maitland, FL: Xulon, 2004.

Lombard, Emile. *De la Glossolalie Chez les Premiers Chrétiens et des Phénomènes Similaires: Étude d'Exégèse et de Psychologie.* G. Bridel & Cie., 1910.

Lovekin, A. A. "Glossolalia: A Critical Study of Alleged Origins, the New Testament and the Early Church." Master's thesis, University of the South, 1962.

MacArthur, John F. *Strange Fire: The Danger of Offending the Holy Spirit with Counterfeit Worship.* Nashville: Thomas Nelson, 2013.

Macchia, Frank D. "Groans Too Deep for Words: Towards a Theology of Tongues as Initial Evidence." *Asian Journal of Pentecostal Studies* 1.2 (1998) 149–73.

———. "Sighs Too Deep for Words: Toward a Theology of Glossolalia." *Journal of Pentecostal Theology* 1.1 (1992) 47–73.

———. *Baptized in the Spirit: A Global Pentecostal Theology.* Grand Rapids: Zondervan, 2006.

———. "The Question of Tongues as Initial Evidence: A Review of Initial Evidence, Edited by Gary B. McGee." *Journal of Pentecostal Theology* 1.2 (1993) 117–27.

Mackie, Alexander. *The Gift of Tongues: A Study in Pathological Aspects of Christianity.* Whitefish, MT: Kessinger, 1921.

Marbell, Bernard E. "The Purpose of Speaking in Tongues in Acts 10:1–48." ThM diss., Dallas Theological Seminary, 1988.

Martyr, Justin. *Dialogue with Trypho.* Cleveland: Beloved, 2015.

May, Jordan Daniel. *Global Witnesses to Pentecost: The Testimony of "Other Tongues."* Cleveland: Centre for Pentecostal Theology, 2013.

McGee, Gary. "The New World of Realities in Which We Live: How Speaking in Tongues Empowered Early Pentecostals." *Pneuma* 30.1 (2008) 108–35.

Menzies, Robert P. *Empowered for Witness: The Spirit in Luke-Acts.* New York: T. & T. Clark International, 2004.

———. *Pentecost: This is Our Story.* Springfield, MO: Gospel, 2013.

———. *Speaking in Tongues: Jesus and the Apostolic Church as Models for the Church Today.* Cleveland: CPT, 2016.

Metaxas, Eric. *Martin Luther: The Man Who Rediscovered God and Changed the World.* New York: Viking, 2017.

Miller, Denzil R. *Missionary Tongues Revisited: More than an Evidence.* Springfield, MO: Pneuma Life, 2013.

Mills, Watson E. *A Theological/Exegetical Approach to Glossolalia.* Lanham, MD: University Press of America, 1962.

———. *Speaking in Tongues: A Guide to Research.* Grand Rapids: Eerdmans, 1986.

Moltmann, Jurgen. *The Spirit of Life: A Universal Affirmation.* Minneapolis: Fortress, 1992.

Morton, Russell. "Gifts in the Context of Love: Reflections on 1 Corinthians 13." *Ashland Theological Journal* 31 (1999) 11–24. https://www.biblicalstudies.org.uk/pdf/ashland_theological_journal/31-1_011.pdf.

Motley, Michael T. "A Linguistic Analysis of Glossolalia: Evidence of Unique Psycholinguistic Processing." *Communication Quarterly* 30.1 (1981) 18–27.

Nelson, P. C. *The Baptism in the Holy Spirit*. Fort Worth, TX: Southwestern, 1942.

Newbigin, Lesslie. *The Open Secret: An Introduction to the Theology of Mission*. Grand Rapids: Eerdmans, 1995.

Osser, H. A., et al. "Glossolalic Speech from a Psycholinguistic Perspective." *Journal of Psycholinguistic Research* 2.1 (1973) 9–19.

Pattison, E. Mansell. "Behavioral Science Research on the Nature of Glossolalia." *Journal of the American Scientific Affiliation* 20.3 (1968) 73–86.

Pelikan, Jaroslav. *The Emergence of the Catholic Tradition (100–600)*. Vol. 1 of *The Christian Tradition: A History of the Development of Doctrine*. Chicago: University of Chicago Press, 2018.

Polhill, John B. *Acts: An Exegetical and Theological Exposition of Holy Scripture*. The New American Commentary 26. Nashville: Broadman, 1992.

Poloma, Margaret M. "Glossolalia, Liminality and Empowered Kingdom Building—A Sociological Perspective." In *Speaking in Tongues: Multi-Disciplinary Perspectives*, edited by Mark J. Cartledge, 147–73. Waynesboro, GA: Paternoster, 2016.

Pomerville, Paul A. *The Third Force in Missions: A Pentecostal Contribution to Contemporary Mission Theology*. Peabody, MA: Hendrickson, 2016.

Resnik, David B. *The Ethics of Research with Human Subjects: Protecting People, Advancing Science, Promoting Trust*. New York: Springer, 2018.

Roberts, Alexander, and James Donaldson, eds. *The Writings of Tertullian*. Vol. 1. Vol. 11 of *Translations of the Writings of the Fathers Down to A. D. 325*. Ante-Nicene Christian Library. Edinburgh: T. & T. Clark, 1869. Reprint, Cambridge, MA: Andover-Harvard Theological Library, 1910.

———. *Tertullianus against Marcion*. Vol. 7 of *Translations of the Writings of the Fathers Down to A. D. 325*. Ante-Nicene Christian Library. Edinburgh: T. & T. Clark, 1868. Reprint, n.p.: Elibron Classics, 2006.

Rotter, Julian B. "Generalized Expectancies for Internal versus External Control of Reinforcement." *Psychological Monographs: General and Applied* 80.1 (1966) 1.

Samarin, William J. "Glossolalia as Learned Behavior." *Canadian Journal of Theology* 15 (1969) 60–64.

———. "Variation and Variables in Religious Glossolalia." *Language in Society* 1 (1972) 121–30.

Schaff, Philip, and Henry Wace, eds. *A Select Library of Nicene and Post-Nicene Fathers of the Christian Church*. 28 vols. [Buffalo: The Christian Literature Company?], 1886–89. Reprint, Peabody, MA: Hendrickson, 1994.

Searle, John R. *Speech Acts: An Essay in the Philosophy of Language*. Cambridge: Cambridge University Press, 1969.

Smith, James K. A. *Thinking in Tongues: Pentecostal Contributions to Christian Philosophy*. Grand Rapids: Eerdmans, 2010.

———. "Tongues as Resistance Discourse." In *Speaking in Tongues: Multi-Disciplinary Perspectives*, edited by Mark J Cartledge, 87–110. Eugene, OR: Wipf & Stock, 2012.

Stagg, Frank E., et al. *Glossolalia: Tongue Speaking in Biblical, Historical, and Psychological Perspective*. Nashville: Abingdon, 1967.

Stephenson, Christopher A. *Types of Pentecostal Theology: Method, System, Spirit*. New York: Oxford University Press, 2013.

Stronstad, Roger. "On Being Baptized in the Holy Spirit: A Lukan Emphasis." In *Trajectories in the Book of Acts: Essays in Honor of John Wesley Wyckoff*, edited by Paul Alexander et al., 160–93. Eugene, OR: Wipf & Stock, 2010.

———. *The Charismatic Theology of St. Luke: Trajectories from the Old Testament to Luke-Acts.* Grand Rapids: Baker Academic, 2012.

Stuhlmacher, Peter. *Historical Criticism and Theological Interpretation of Scripture: Toward a Hermeneutics of Consent.* Eugene, OR: Wipf & Stock, 1977.

Torrance, Thomas F. *Reality and Evangelical Theology: The Realism of Christian Revelation.* Downers Grove, IL: InterVarsity, 1999.

Unger, Merrill F. *New Testament Teachings on Tongues.* Grand Rapids: Kregel, 1971.

Unnik, Willem C. van. "Luke-Acts, a Storm Center in Contemporary Scholarship." In *Evangelia, Paulina, Acta*, 92–110. Pt. 1 of *Sparsa collecta*. Novum Testamentum, Supplements 29. Boston: Brill, 1973.

Vondey, Wolfgang. *Pentecostal Theology: Living the Full Gospel.* New York: T. & T. Clark International, 2018.

Vreeland, Derek. "Edward Irving: Preacher, Prophet & Charismatic Theologian." *Pneuma Review* 5.2 (2002) 1–10.

Walter, Yoshija, et al. "Brain Structural Evidence for a Frontal Pole Specialization in Glossolalia." *IBRO Reports* 9 (2020) 32–36.

Warrington, Keith. *Pentecostal Theology: A Theology of Encounter.* New York: T. & T. Clark International, 2008.

Williams, George H., and Edith Waldvogel. "A History of Speaking in Tongues and Related Gifts." In *The Charismatic Movement*, edited by M. P. Hamilton, 61–113. Grand Rapids: Eerdmans, 1975.

Williams, John Rodman. *Renewal Theology: Systematic Theology from a Charismatic Perspective.* Grand Rapids: HarperCollins, 1995.

Wyckoff, John W. "The Baptism in the Holy Spirit." In *Systematic Theology*, edited by Stanley M. Horton, 423–55. Springfield, MO: Gospel, 1995.

———. "Charismatic Ministry in St. Luke's Theology." In *Reading St. Luke's Text and Theology: Pentecostal Voices: Essays in Honor of Professor Roger Stronstad*, edited by R. P. Tuppurainen, 147–58. Eugene, OR: Pickwick, 2019.

Yong, Amos. *The Spirit Poured Out on All Flesh: Pentecostalism and the Possibility of Global Theology.* Grand Rapids: Baker Academic, 2005.

———. "Academic Glossolalia? Pentecostal Scholarship, Multi-disciplinarity, and the Science-Religion Conversation." *Journal of Pentecostal Theology* 14.1 (2005) 61–80.

———. *Renewing Christian Theology: Systematics for a Global Christianity.* Waco, TX: Baylor University Press, 2014.

———. *The Missiological Spirit: Christian Mission Theology in the Third Millennium Global Context.* Cambridge: James Clarke & Co., 2014.

———. *Mission after Pentecost: The Witness of the Spirit from Genesis to Revelation.* Grand Rapids: Baker Academics, 2019.

Made in the USA
Coppell, TX
02 December 2021